SOUTH FORK PLACE NAMES

NOVELS BY WILLIAM MULVIHILL

Fire Mission

The Mantrackers

The Sands of Kalahari

Night of the Axe

I've Got Viktor Schalkenburg

God Is Blind

Boyfriend

Serengeti

The Tiger Heart

Meadow Lane

Sagaponack

Ava

SOUTH FORK PLACE NAMES

SOME INFORMAL LONG ISLAND HISTORY

WILLIAM P. MULVIHILL

BRICKILN PRESS
SAG HARBOR, NEW YORK

South Fork Place Names
William Mulvihill
Copyright © 2007 Brickiln Press, LLC

All rights reserved. No part of this book may be reproduced (except for inclusion in reviews), disseminated or utilized in any form or by any means, electronic or mechanical, including photocopying, recording, or in any information storage and retrieval system, or the Internet/World Wide Web without written permission from Brickiln Press.

For further information, please contact:

Brickiln Press, LLC
P.O. Box 2772
Sag Harbor, New York 11963

Book design by:
VMC Art & Design LLC
www.vmc-artdesign.com

Cover Photograph by William Mulvihill
Author's Photograph by Nancy Mulvihill
Interior Photographs by Mary Ann and Daniel Mulvihill-Decker unless otherwise noted.

Printed in the United States of America
Printed by McNaughton & Gunn, Inc.
Printed on 100% Recycled Paper

Library of Congress Control Number: 95-077332
ISBN 978-0-9795018-0-7

Fifth Edition printed in 2010

Mulvihill, William (1923-2004),
History,
Long Island

I dedicate this collection

of place names to future historians

and to William Wallace Tooker (1848-1917)

of Sag Harbor whose invaluable book

on Long Island Indian Place Names

sparked my original interest

in this subject.

"Inhabitants of Long Island!

Remember your high descent and

emulate the example of your pious ancestors."
—Nathan Prime

"...Isle of sweet brooks and

drinking water, healthy air and soil!

Isle of the salty shore and breeze and brine."
—Walt Whitman, *Paumanok*

"For many good reasons

it is desirable that the

old name-places be preserved."
—Harry D. Sleight

"A writer must recite the names

of place much the way a mother

says the names of her children."
—Yeats

CONTENTS

ACKNOWLEDGEMENTS	i
FOREWORD BY RICHARD F. WELCH	iii
INTRODUCTION	vi
SHINNECOCK	1
SOUTHAMPTON	11
NORTH SEA	33
WATER MILL	45
SAG HARBOR AND NOYAC	55
NORTH HAVEN	99
BRIDGEHAMPTON AND SAGAPONACK	107
NORTHWEST	123
EAST HAMPTON	133
SPRINGS	159
AMAGANSETT AND NAPEAGUE	171
MONTAUK	183
ISLANDS	205
EAST END HISTORICAL SOCIETIES AND MUSEUMS	219
SOURCES	227
INDEX OF PLACE NAMES	231

ACKNOWLEDGEMENTS

Our father, Bill Mulvihill, loved corresponding with a remarkably large number of people who contributed to his knowledge base about local name origins. They are listed under *Sources* in the back of this book and to each and every one of them we are very grateful.

Our heartfelt thanks go out to all those who have helped us to reissue our Dad's book, a work that was exceptionally close to his heart.

Thanks especially to Daniel Mulvihill-Decker who spent countless hours separating the entries geographically, researching many of them and providing moral support at times when the project hit rough spots along the way. Thanks to Kathryn Szoka and Maryann Calendrille for their brainstorming, editorial advice and encouragement and to Jim Monaco for his suggestions regarding production.

Thanks to Richard Welch, historian and close friend of our Dad, for his foreword, his input on many issues regarding the book and especially for his many fact-finding adventures with Dad (usually involving lunch and a cold beer) to research items for this book.

Many thanks to Dolores M. Zebrowski, our Dad's sister, for her endless encouragement to finally republish this very special work.

And finally a very special thanks to our Mom, Mary Marceau Mulvihill, for her proofreading expertise and for her love and support of our Dad and his writing through fifty-eight years of marriage and devotion.

Mary Ann Mulvihill-Decker and Nancy Mulvihill

FOREWORD

Bill Mulvihill (1923-2004) was a man of far-ranging interests whose mysteries he identified, researched, and explicated. While he preferred to think of himself as a novelist, history, either implicitly or explicitly, formed the core of much of his writing, both his fiction and non-fiction. He had a firm command of European and American history and became an authority on Africa long before the subject became fashionable. His vocational and intellectual pursuits merged in his love of books, which he collected. Bill was not snobbish about popular culture. He kept abreast of musical tastes—though he was most fond of jazz—popular fiction, magazines, and movies. Bill was a child of the South Fork, born and raised in Sag Harbor. Though his professional life took him to Nassau County, the area east of the Shinnecock Canal held primacy of place in Bill's affections. Bill returned often to his old neighborhoods, and was owner of a sizeable tract of land off Brickiln Road. In recent years, Bill's love and knowledge of Sag Harbor and the South Fork resulted in a growing volume of work devoted to the area's history and environment. Many of his articles appeared in the *Sag Harbor Express*, though he was also a contributing editor to the *Long Island Forum*, where his work frequently appeared.

Bill's articles were as varied as his interests. They dealt with Sag Harbor mariners, slavery, the Revolutionary War, wayward East Enders in Montana, Victorian poets, and Civil War regiments raised in eastern Suffolk. Additionally, Bill turned out a large number of articles on environmental conservation and wildlife issues—a perennial interest which grew from his love of the land of the South Fork and his efforts to preserve the area's environmental heritage for the future.

Perhaps Bill's most concentrated—certainly his most prolonged—effort was devoted to what he termed "Some informal Long Island history." This was his *South Fork Place Names*, basically a work of homage to the land and places he loved best. *South Fork Place Names* was always a work in progress, expanded, revamped, and rewritten to accommodate new entries and fresh information. The first edition appeared in 1994, a spiral-bound booklet produced at a local photocopying store. Bill upgraded the book both in terms of content and production values, contracting with professional printers for his later printings. Three subsequent editions were produced while Bill was alive. Each appeared in soft cover format, with the newer volumes containing more information or listings than the previous.

Bill gleaned his information from a variety of sources. He

consulted many of the standard texts on Long Island history, questioned local historians, both professional and amateur, kept an eye out for information in newspapers, and often asked someone to check out a background fact. One of his pleasures, or diversions as he liked to say, was driving around the roads and byways of the East End, popping down unmarked lanes, exploring nature preserves and trails, stopping to take in historic sites, or enjoying the natural beauty so abundant on the Fork. Frequently, a new street sign, house or business name or local name would catch his interest and he'd jot it down for later research. In such ways the entries in *South Fork Place Names* multiplied.

One of Bill's major concerns was to see that much of the land owned by his family since 1920 was preserved in its natural state. Before his death he saw the establishment of The Anna and Daniel Mulvihill Preserve, named after his parents. Two years after his death a large parcel of adjoining land was also designated as a preserve and named The William Mulvihill Preserve. In 2009, another adjoining parcel that Bill had named Clonmoylan Woods after the Irish townland of his paternal grandfather's birth, was similarly protected. The preserves will remain an enduring memorial to his love for the land east of the Shinnecock Canal. It is likely that, in a different, but equally tangible way, so will *South Fork Place Names*. As a man of the written word, Bill would appreciate this.

—Richard F. Welch

INTRODUCTION

Throughout as many years as I can remember, my father, William Mulvihill, would wonder aloud about the names of places. This was true whether on family trips or around the island. But nowhere else captured his interest and imagination as did the South Fork of Long Island. Born and raised in Sag Harbor, his hometown always remained the central and most beloved place on earth for him. His thirst for learning about its past was unquenchable.

As a boy exploring his native forests and wetlands, he often found arrowheads and other artifacts. This began a lifelong interest in those who came before him and in the heritage of the entire area. The South Fork still contains a wealth of Native American place names, many of which are discussed in this book and which echo of a time so different from ours, but not very long ago.

After a thirty-four year career as a high school history teacher, he took to his many personal writing projects with even greater passion. One of these has been compiling the several previous editions of this book, published prior to his death in 2004. The additions to the text in this printing are his, with several exceptions, as he had already collected many new entries for the next edition when he suddenly took ill. He also chose to add graphics to the work. Shortly before he died, he asked me to update his work for this edition. Our family chose to add photos, the foreword and to separate the entries geographically.

Through his exploration of local name origins, he enlivens story after story of South Fork history. It is a history rich with color and texture, of native inhabitants, of shipwrecks, of wild animals and plant life, of sea captains and whalers, of soldiers and intrigue, of immigrants, settlers, artists, actors and writers. His research enriches us all, as we now walk the same roads as those who walked them before us, but with a fresh eye, a new sense of the place names we encounter, the old stories we recall.

—Mary Ann Mulvihill-Decker

SOUTH FORK PLACE NAMES

SHINNECOCK

ART VILLAGE

Now a residential area north of the Shinnecock Indian Reservation in Southampton, west of Tuckahoe Lane. The name derived from an outdoor art school proposed, in the 19th century, by Mrs. William Hoyt, Mrs. Henry Kirk Porter and Samuel Parrish. The Shinnecock Summer School of Art (1892) was headed by the artist William Merritt Chase (1849-1916) who summered in Shinnecock Hills in a house designed by Stanford White.

BAYBERRY LAND

A 307-acre estate and opulent mansion designed by Walter and Eliot Cross, built in 1917 by John Corrigan for Charles Hamilton Sabin (once president of the Guarantee Trust Company) and once the nexus of Southampton society. It's on the north side of Sebonic Road and extends to Great Peconic Bay, Cold Spring Pond and the National Golf Links of America. Cold Spring Road runs through the property. The estate and gardens were laid out by Marion C. Coffin.

Bayberry (Wax Myrtle) is a common shrub which produces a berry-like fruit, covered with wax and is used in making candles.

CANOE PLACE

The Shinnecock (Sinnecox) Indians dug a narrow canal—in the area now called Shinnecock—to allow canoes to pass from Peconic Bay to Shinnecock Bay. In 1640, a deed was signed by the original settlers—Howell, Needham, Halsey, Cooper, etc.—and Indian leaders which gave ownership from "where the Indians hayle over their canoes out of the North bay to the south side of the Island to the English of lands lying eastward"; that is the South Fork. In exchange the English gave goods and a promise to defend the local Indians from "unjust violence" from other Indians. In 1885 dredging began to expand the narrow canal to accommodate sea-going ships.

CHURCH OF ALL ANGELS

Nonexistent since April 3, 1905 when the church, built in 1894, was destroyed by fire. A large stone identifies the site west of Depot Road and east of Hills Station Road in Southampton's Shinnecock Hills.

CIRCASSIAN MEMORIAL

At the Shinnecock Church in the Shinnecock Indian Reservation. Here, on a small granite monument, are the names of the 10 men (of 28) who died on December 30, 1876 when the ship *Circassian* stranded on a bar off Bridgehampton, broke apart in an icy gale.

COLD SPRING POND

A Town Proprietor's map shows that this body of water was called Cold Spring Bay—open to Great Peconic Bay—in 1653 and was part of the Seaponack Meadow Division in Shinnecock Hills. *Seaponack*, an Indian name, evolved into Sebonic.

FISH CROW LANDING

Spelled Fishcow Landing on most maps of the Shinnecock Indian Reservation in Southampton. This is an ideal habitat for the Fish Crow (*Corvus ossifragus*) which hunts the shallows and mudflats for carrion, clams and fiddler crabs.

GOOD GROUND

The original name for Hampton Bays, so named because it was an oasis of rich topsoil within the sandy soil of the Pine Barrens. The South Fork starts here.

HILLS STATION ROAD

Named for the former Shinnecock Railroad Station that, in 1887, was built in the Shinnecock Hills by Austin Corbin.

LENAPE ROAD

Runs south from the Montauk Highway to the bay in Shinnecock Hills. Delaware Indians, some of whom migrated to Long Island, called themselves *Leni Lenape* or *Lenape*, "the people."

MILL HILL MILL

Now known as the Southampton College Mill on the campus of Southampton College. Originally this windmill stood in the heart of the village near Windmill Lane. Built in the early 1700s, it was, in 1890, moved to its present site. Once owned by Arthur B. Claflin, it passed (with his mansion) to new owners to become the Tucker Mill Inn. Tennessee Williams rented the mill for a summer and wrote there. In 1962 the mill with the rest of the property became Southampton College.

NATIONAL GOLF LINKS OF AMERICA

Charles Blair Macdonald (1872-1927) was an American who

attended Saint Andrews University in Scotland where he fell in love with the charms of golf. He became a top-flight player and America's first important golf course architect. He created this course for The National Golf Links of America, a corporation. It opened in 1911 and is contiguous to the Shinnecock Golf Club, Bullhead Bay and Great Peconic Bay.

Macdonald's Mansion, Ballyshear, is off White's Lane in North Sea.

OLD FORT POND

The bay west of the Shinnecock Indian Reservation in Southampton. Abigail Fithian Halsey wrote that during the British occupation of Long Island, soldiers "threw up earthworks west of the village, marked today as the Old Fort."

Also, Old Fort Landing.

OSCEOLA DRIVE

A road leading from the Montauk Highway into the Shinnecock Indian Reservation. Osceola was a Seminole chief in Florida, not a local Indian with historical significance.

PECONIC

For two bodies of water between the North and South Forks, the Great and Little Peconic Bays, there appears to be no agreement by the early scholars as to the precise Indian word and its meaning. Tooker concludes an exhaustive discourse on linguistic variants by saying that it might be translated as a "small field." There is also no precise knowledge of where the field or locality or Indian village was originally located.

REBADAM LANE

South of the Montauk Highway close to the Indian Reservation. The name (accent on the first syllable) comes from Reba Adam who once lived in the area.

SCOTCH MIST LANE

A road through Shinnecock Hills in Southampton and close to the Scotch Mist Inn which was destroyed by fire. Scotch mist is "a thick soaking mist characteristic of the Scottish hills" which is not uncommon in this area.

SEBONAC NECK

Land on Peconic Bay in Shinnecock Hills in Southampton, between Cold Spring Pond and Bullhead Bay. The Indian origin of the word—*Seaponack*—similar to Sagaponack, refers to ground-nuts or tubers or perhaps the roots of the yellow lily which is supposed to resemble the sweet potato and was prized by the Indians, who had a stockaded village here.

The eastern part of the neck is now The National Golf Links of America. The western part is Bayberry Land, an estate.

Native elders at Annual Shinnecock Indian Powwow
Photo courtesy of the Shinnecock Nation

SHINNECOCK

A bay, hills, a neck of land and a canal in western Southampton. The word was first used in 1641 referring to "shinecock plaine." Tooker tells us that the Indian word meant "at the level land."

The Shinnecocks were Algonquin and inhabited the area of Southampton. The Montauks held the far east of the South Fork and the Manhassets ruled Shelter Island.

SHINNECOCK HILLS GOLF CLUB

At Southampton and on the National Register of Historic Places. Built in 1891 as the first clubhouse for golf players.

Designed by McKim, Mead and White. One president was Samuel Parrish.

SHINNECOCK HILLS PRESERVE

Once part of the golf course, these 26-acres are, since 1994, a Nature Conservancy holding, valuable as a site of maritime grassland. Bounded by St. Andrews Road (the preserve entrance) and south by the railroad tracks. Look for bushy rockrose, shadbush and beach plum.

SHINNECOCK INDIAN RESERVATION

Once called Shinnecock Neck, leased back to the Indians in 1703 and sold to them in 1862 by the Proprietors of Southampton. Surrounded by the waters of Shinnecock Bay and bounded north by the Montauk Highway. This property is the home of people who claim Shinnecock ancestry. They are recognized by the state of New York as an authentic Indian tribe. Recognition by the federal government is now pending, preliminary approval having been granted.

SQUAW HILL

Part of the Shinnecock Hills near Tuckahoe. Squaw is derived from the Indian word *escqua,* for female. We can speculate that the hill, like Squaw Island in South Oyster Bay, was a refuge for women and children in times of war.

ST. ANDREW'S ROAD

Runs from Tuckahoe Road in Shinnecock Hills to cross the North Highway to Montauk Highway. Charles Blair MacDonald, the architect of the National Golf Links of America, attended St. Andrew's University in Scotland in 1873-1874 and fell in love with golf on the famous golf course.

STUDIO LANE

Off Montauk Highway and runs to Tuckahoe Lane. Named for the studio of William Merritt Chase (1849-1916) which became the focal point of Art Village and the Shinnecock Summer School of Art (1892).

SUGAR LOAF HILL

In Shinnecock Hills off the Montauk Highway. The hundred-foot high bluff affords an unbroken view of Shinnecock Bay. Also, Sugar Loaf Road.

TUCKER MILL INN

Nonexistent but the building is now the Administrative Center of Southampton College. Built by Arthur B. Claflin in the Shinnecock Hills as a private 30-room home. This Italian style house was furnished from items from a European castle. Originally called Heathmere it was transformed into an inn by restaurateur Tucker and his artist wife.

The adjacent 18th century windmill adds to its name.

SOUTHAMPTON

AGAWAM

The 60-acre town pond of Southampton. William Wallace Tooker's research led him to believe that the Algonquin word means "low flat meadows that are frequently inundated." Once a marshy area called Job's Swamp. Agawam Park at the foot of Job's Lane covers five acres.

ATTERBURY ROAD

Grosvenor Atterbury (1869-1956) was a prominent architect and town planner. He graduated from Yale and studied painting with William Merritt Chase and once worked for

McKim, Mead and White. He completed his training in Paris at the *École des Beau Arts*.

In Southampton he created many large country homes. He created the Parrish Art Museum (1913) and did many commissions for the Russell Sage Foundation and the Metropolitan Museum of Art.

His Southampton home (next to the house of S.L. Parrish) was close to Atterbury Road off the Montauk Highway opposite Hills Station Road.

BISHOP'S LANE

In Southampton Village and named for Charles Bishop who once owned land on the west side of the byway.

BOWDEN SQUARE

In Southampton Village. Livingston Bowden was an original subscriber to the incorporation of Southampton in 1894. The Square is off Main Street.

BOWER'S LANE

A short byway connecting Flying Point Road and David White's Lane. Bower is a very old Southampton family name. Around 1648 Jonas Bower built a house (still standing) at 126 Main Street lived in by three generations of the family.

BOYESEN ROAD

Links Captain's Neck Lane with Halsey Neck Lane in Southampton Village. Named for Professor H.H. Boyesen who owned property here in 1894. A five-acre lot here was sold to John Halsey in 1752.

BREESE LANE

In 1895, James L. Breese hired his friend Stanford White to build a mansion (The Orchard) on his 30 acres on Hill Street in Southampton. Breese, a man of opulent tastes, made and lost several fortunes. When he died, at eighty, his young girlfriend committed suicide.

Breese Lane runs north of Hill Street in Southampton Village.

CAPTAIN'S NECK

The land known as Captain's Neck in Southampton was bought sometime before 1651 by two brothers who were whaling captains, Hubert White and Elias White. Thirty-one acres of the southern portion of this property are now a Nature Conservancy holding—The Ruth Wales DuPont Sanctuary.

COOPER'S FARM ROAD

Off Windmill Road in Southampton and named for the 40-acre farm of Captain Mercator Cooper. The Greek Revival house, built in 1805 by Mercator's father, is now called Cooper Hall.

It has three stories, seventeen rooms and a widow's walk. Owned by the local library.

COOPER'S NECK LANE

Close to Cooper's Neck Pond (once called Meadowmere Pond) in Southampton. Cooper is an original (1640) settler name.

Mercator Cooper, a whaling captain, sailed his ship *Manhattan* into a Japanese port in 1845 in order to return Japanese castaways. This visit pre-dated Commodore Perry's historic "opening of Japan" eight years later.

CRYDER LANE

A short road in Southampton Village, east of First Neck Road dead-ending at the ocean beach. Named for the Duncan Cryder family, early summer visitors.

The Cryder Memorial window, *Sir Galahad*, in Saint Andrew's Dune Church was created in 1902 by Louis Comfort Tiffany.

CULVER HILL

In Southampton Village where Culver Street joins Pond Lane with First Neck Lane. Once called Margaret's Hill for Margaret LeBarr, an Acadian who in 1755 came to the Village from Canada, and lived in a house overlooking Job's Lane. Later called Culver Hill after Gershom Culver.

DANZ ROAD

Named for Vincent Danz, Southampton High School graduate, a New York City policeman who lost his life in the terrorist attack on the World Trade Center. The road is a beach access way (Road D) off Meadow Lane.

DAVID WHITE'S LANE

In Southampton Village north off the Montauk Highway, running to the Edge of the Woods Road. White is a 17th century name. In 1805 a large farm in the vicinity was sold to William White who left it to his son, David White.

FIRST NECK LANE

In Southampton and was, in the early days, the first lane west of Agawam Lake, connecting Hill Street and Dune Road. Now an area of large estates.

FORDHAM ROAD

Off Hill Street in Southampton west of Breese Lane. Reverend Robert Fordham settled in the village around 1649, the first of a widespread and illustrious family. In Sag Harbor, Fordham Street runs off the Bridgehampton Sag Harbor turnpike to Brickiln Road.

FOSTER STREET

Off South Main Street in Southampton. The Fosters were

original settlers on the South Fork and produced many distinguished men and women. John Foster was a co-owner with Joseph Conkling of the first (1760) Sag Harbor ship to seek whales on the high seas.

FOWLER STREET

In Southampton, running from Wickapogue Road to the ocean. Jesse Fowler once had a farm in the vicinity.

RICHARD L. FOWLER NATURE WALK

South of Wickapoque Road in Southampton opposite Narrow Lane. A path leads to nine-acre Wickapoque Pond.

A bronze plaque reads:

> *Richard L. Fowler Nature Walk.*
> *In memory of and gratitude for the years of*
> *dedicated service to the residents of Southampton.*
> *1968-1985.*

GARY MAC'S WAY

In 2004, Beach Access Road F off Meadow Lane in Southampton was renamed to honor Gary McNamara, a local coach to many youngsters.

GIN LANE

A gin is an old English name for corral or trap for stray livestock, cattle, goats, and pigs. The enclosure had a gate that swung inward to the trap but not outward. Gin Lane, in Southampton, opened in 1664, was named because of a gin fence in the locality. The road was extended to include a part of Meadow Lane.

GREAT PLAINS ROAD

In Southampton Village between Captain's Neck Lane and First Neck Lane. Pelletreau wrote that "The Great Plaines is the tract bounded North by Hill Street, or Road to Shinnecock Hills, east by Town Pond, (Agawam Lake) west by Head of the Creek, (Heady Creek) south by the Beach." It was laid out in ten-acre lots before 1670.

HALSEY HOMESTEAD

On South Main Street in Southampton and open to the public under the auspices of the local historical museum. Built around 1660 by Thomas Halsey, it may be the oldest frame house in the state of New York and is recognized by the National Trust for Historic Preservation.

Silas Halsey (1718-1786) soldiered in the Revolution.

Silas Halsey (1743-1832) served in Congress as did his sons Nicoll Halsey (1782-1865) and Jehiel Howard Halsey (1788-1867).

HALSEY NECK LANE

Named after David Halsey (1663-1731), this Southampton

road connects Hill Street and Dune Road and is close to Halsey Neck Pond. There is also a Halsey Lane in Water Mill. The Halsey family is one of the oldest and most distinguished on the South Fork. In 1817, a whaling ship, the *Argonaut*, captained by Eliphalet Halsey negotiated the dangerous waters off Cape Horn, the first Sag Harbor ship to enter the Pacific. Doctor Seymore Halsey served as surgeon in the Mexican War with the First Mississippi Rifles which was commanded by Jefferson Davis. Nine Halsey men from Bridgehampton served in the Civil War, in which three died.

HEADY CREEK

The name of this area in Southampton Village was originally Head of the Creek after the inlet west of Captain's Neck Lane and east of the Shinnecock Indian Reservation. This body of water eventually took the name of Heady Creek. Heady Creek Lane runs off Lee Avenue at the northern part of the creek.

HERRICK STREET

Between Main Street and Old Town Road in Southampton. A 1710 deed to George Herrick shows that it was left to his son Captain James Herrick.

HILL STREET

Named for Mill Hill, the site of an 18th century windmill. Once called Shinnecock Road, named because it was the way from Southampton Village to Shinnecock Hills.

HORSE MILL LANE

In Southampton, a now-vanished road that ran to Lake Agawam. Built around 1763, it was so named because a horse-powered mill was built there around 1700. Also, Horsemill Lane in Mecox.

HOWELL STREET

Edward Howell was the leader of the original settlers, who in 1640, landed at North Sea. Nathaniel Howell, Jr. (1742-1809) was an officer in the Revolution serving in Colonel Josiah Smith's (1723-1786) New York Regiment of Minute Men (Suffolk County). John E. Howell is remembered on the Broken Mast Monument in Sag Harbor's Oakland Cemetery. In 1840, as Master of the *France*, "he lost his life in an encounter with a sperm whale in the Pacific." He was 27. Captain Nathan Howell in 1832 built the Howell-Napier house at 52 Main Street in Sag Harbor.

A widespread and distinguished South Fork family. George Rogers Howell was, in the 19th century, Southampton town historian. Howell Street is in Southampton Village.

HUNTING STREET

In Southampton, named for a distinguished East End family, whose roots go back to John Huntting, born in England in 1602. Benjamin Huntting, in 1785, was co-owner of one of the first whale ships; a later voyage by the brig *Lucy* reached

Brazil. In 1846, he built an elegant house designed by Minard Lafever that became the summer residence of Mrs. Russell Sage and is now the Sag Harbor Whaling Museum.

Henry Huntting was killed at Jackson, Mississippi, January 2, 1864 serving with the 4th Illinois Cavalry.

JAGGER LANE

A Southampton road named for John Jagger who, in the 1650s, arrived from Stamford, Connecticut, as one of the original settlers. Now a widespread and illustrious family on Long Island. Oscar Jagger was cited for bravery at Devaux Neck in South Carolina in Civil War service with the 127th New York Volunteer Regiment.

JOB'S LANE

An original 1640 Southampton settler, Job Sayre owned land in the vicinity of the Parrish Art Museum. A path here, created by cows, became known as Job's Lane. Once called Academy Lane when The Southampton Academy stood on the former site of the Rogers Memorial Library.

In Bridgehampton, another Job's Lane (1726) runs from Mecox Road to Dune Road on the ocean.

JULE POND

In Wickapogue close to the ocean, west of Channel Pond.

On Beers map of 1894 it's called "Capt. Tommy's Pond." A "Captain T. Sayre" owned land in this area.

KEEWAYDIN

In Longfellow's *The Song of Hiawatha* (1854), *Keewaydin* is the Indian name for the northwest wind. It was chosen to name the ten-acre estate on Halsey Neck in Southampton. Stanford White (1853-1906) designed the twenty room house in 1892.

LEE AVENUE

J. Bowers Lee, an early summer resident in Southampton, owned a house on a large parcel extending south from Hill Street, bordered on the west by Heady Creek. The house was destroyed by fire, the parcel developed but the name remains. It was once called Head-O-Creek Road.

LINDEN LANE

Runs from Southampton's South Main Street to Agawam Lake. In 1842, the French ship *Louis Philippe* was wrecked on the beach at Mecox. To lighten the ship many trees and shrubs were thrown overboard. The ship was saved and many trees and shrubs drifted ashore and were also saved— "beech, laburnum and linden trees", according to Jeanette Edwards Rattray. It's possible that Linden Lane is named for those sea-soaked European trees that survived to find life in Long Island soil.

LITTLE PLAINS ROAD

"The Little Plain," wrote Pelletreau, "is on the south side of Gin Lane, at the south end of Main Street in Southampton." The name might have been given to this tract of land to distinguish it from the Great Plains on the western side of Agawam Lake. Little Plains Road now runs south from the Montauk Highway to Gin Lane. The Little Plain was laid out in 1656.

LOLA PRENTICE PARK

In Southampton, adjacent to Windmill Lane. During the British occupation of Southampton (1777-1778) there was a fort here. The name's origin is unknown.

MAGEE STREET

A street in Southampton named for an Ireland-born blacksmith, James Magee, who lived there in the 18th century.

THE MEADOW CLUB

Mrs. Frederic Betts and Mrs. Albert Buck lived in ocean-front homes in Southampton and would meet in a nearby meadow each Saturday for tea. They invited friends and moved their meetings to another meadow. Eventually, this land was bought from Dr. T. Gaillard who built the first summer home on the dunes. In 1887, the Meadow Club was built.

MEADOW LANE

While no meadows exist here in the modern sense—greenswards ripe with tall grass—this peninsula in Southampton fronting on the ocean did provide good pasture in the early days. Along Shinnecock Bay there were unbroken stretches of *Spartina patens* (salt hay), aquatic plants rich in nutrients. Cattle turned loose here needed no attention. A shut fence (or gin) could keep them penned in on the long peninsula.

MEETING HOUSE LANE

Southampton's early settlers built in 1641 a meeting house on the land now occupied by the Southampton Hospital. The meeting house was used as a place of worship, for town meetings and as a court house. When a new church was built, the town gave the building to Richard Mills, "to keep an ordinary tavern for diet and lodging."

MOSES LANE

Off Hill Street in Southampton. Named for Moses Culver. The family name is mentioned as early as 1698 in a deed from Isaac Halsey to Gersham Culver at "a place called Ox Pasture."

MOUNTAIN LAUREL ROAD

Off Sandy Hollow Road in Southampton. *Kalmia latifolia* is named for botanist Peter Kalm, a Swedish student of

Linnaeus, who came to North America in the 18th century and was so impressed by the beauty of the flower that he introduced it to Europe where it is more esteemed than on the South Fork.

MUNN POINT

Marshlands on the north side of Meadow Lane in Southampton village. The property is named in honor of Orson D. Munn, a village trustee and parks commissioner from 1967-1985. A 650-foot walkway runs to Shinnecock Bay.

Munn's Pond was created in 1925 by Carolyn Nunder Munn when she built a dam across a small creek. It's now the southernmost end of Sears Bellow County Park just west of Hampton Bays.

MURRAY LANE

In Southampton Village off Old Town Road near Wickapogue Pond. Named for the Murrays, one of the earliest families to create a summer colony in the area.

OLD FIELD LANE

Abigail Fithian Halsey mentions a John Ouldfields who was a tanner in Southampton in 1651. Old Field Lane leads south from Hill Street. Also Old Field Road close to Conscience Point at North Sea.

OLD FORT

On Windmill Lane in Southampton Village at Lola Prentice Memorial Park. A plaque reads:

> *The Old Fort site of old British fort erected during English occupation of Southampton 1777-78.*

OLD SOUTHAMPTON BURIAL GROUND

On the west side of Little Plains Road in Southampton. Also called South End Burial Ground. The first burial was in 1649. Many gravestones are for Howells and Herricks.

OLD TOWN ROAD

Old Town was the original (1640) settlement at Southampton. Old Town Road was Southampton's first street which, according to Abigail Halsey, must have been east of Old Town Pond and ran to the ocean. The Howells and Piersons were early Puritan settler families from Massachusetts who built simple houses in this locality, planted their crops and survived to create the village.

OSBORNE AVENUE

Off 27A in the Village of Southampton. The original Osbornes left England in 1620 and settled in Connecticut. Some members moved to East Hampton. In 1775 Jeremiah

Osborne signed the Declaration of Independence. An ancient, widespread and distinguished family of the South Fork.

OX PASTURE ROAD

A road in Southampton Village extending from Agawam Lake to Heady Creek in the vicinity of lands used by the early settlers to pasture oxen and cattle; part of the land was reserved for the use of the minister and was referred to as parsonage land. Once called The Road to Captains Neck.

PARRISH MEMORIAL HALL

On Herrick Road and, since 1942, owned by Southampton Hospital. Grosvenor Atterbury was the architect and used rounded, swell-belly bricks. A memorial to Southampton men who died in World War One.

PARRISH MUSEUM OF SOUTHAMPTON

Founded in 1897 by Samuel Longstreth Parrish (1843-1932) to house his personal collection of art and to create an arboretum. The building was designed by Grosvenor Atterbury, a distinguished architect who had a summer home west of the village. The garden was designed by Warren Manning. In 1942 the village took ownership from the museum's trustees. Parrish Street is in North Sea.

PELLETREAU STREET

Elias Pelletreau (1726-1810), an apprentice goldsmith in

New York, moved to Southampton. He was elected in 1776 as a militia captain of a formation of old men—some seventy and older in preparation for the Revolution.

Elias soon left Southampton for Connecticut for the duration of the war. Three generations of Pelletreaus were silversmiths and artisans in Southampton.

William S. Pelletreau (1840-1918), a later member of this family, was one of the original historians of the Town of Southampton. Robert H. Pelletreau, a native of Patchogue and descendant of Elias Pelletreau, was the American ambassador to Tunisia who was named to initiate open talks with PLO leaders in 1988.

Pelletreau Street is off David White's Lane in Southampton Village.

PENNIES LANDING

A short road in Southampton Village that is a continuation of Ox Pasture Road ending at Taylor Creek.

The name could be derived from John Pinney, a blacksmith who owned land "in the Ox Pasture" in 1696.

PHILIPS POND

In Wickapogue at Southampton west of Fowler Street and possibly named for Zerubbabel Philips, a very early resident of the area. In 1894 on Beers map it's called Halsey's Pond.

POST CROSSING

Runs from Southampton's North Main Street to Elm Street. A homestead in this area was once owned by Albert J. Post. The historic Post House dates from 1684 and is, after Southampton's Halsey Homestead, the oldest frame house in New York. Another owner of the Post House was Zebulon Jessup who was a major in the Continental Army.

PULASKI STREET

In Southampton Village, west from David White's Lane. Named for Casimir Pulaski (1747-1779) the Polish army officer who came to help George Washington during the Revolution; a general and Chief of Cavalry.

ROGERS MEMORIAL LIBRARY

Harriet Jones Rogers in her will of 1895 left her home on Main Street and ten thousand dollars to create a Southampton Village Library on Job's Lane.

Designed by Robert H. Robertson, since 1999 it is the Carroll Petrie Center for Education.

ROGERS STREET

Off Old Town Road in Southampton Village. William Rogers was an original 1640 settler. Zephaniah Rogers was an officer who marched to Ticonderoga with John Hulbert during the Revolution.

RUTH WALES DUPONT SANCTUARY

The southern tip of Captain's Neck (once called Captain's Point) in Southampton Village, bordering Shinnecock Bay. Acquired in 1961 by The Nature Conservancy, this 31-acre preserve (including Ephram's Point) is mostly marshland which, in early years, was valuable as a source of Spartina grass, a food for livestock.

SANFORD STREET

Off Major's Path and named for an early and distinguished family. Nathan Sanford (1777-1833) was a state assemblyman and state senator, a member of the U.S. Senate and, in 1824, ran for vice president.

SOUTHAMPTON

The Indian name was *Agawam*: "a place abounding with fish." Some sources suggest that most of the original New England colonists of 1640 had ancestral roots in Southampton, England and named it after that place which was an ancient Roman city called *Hamtun* and *Suhampton*. Another source claims that it was named in honor of Henry Wriothesly, the Earl of Southampton in England who had been a director and treasurer of the Virginia Company, a well-known and respected figure in the New World of the 17th century. See plaque at the junction of Wickapogue Road and Old Town Road.

SOUTHAMPTON HISTORICAL MUSEUM

On Meeting House Lane in Southampton Village. Built in 1843 as a private home for Captain Albert Rogers. Sold in 1898 to Samuel Parrish and moved to its present site. Now owned by the village.

ST. ANDREW'S DUNE CHURCH

At the south end of Southampton's Lake Agawam, built on the dunes facing the ocean. Moved inland in 1996 as protection from the surf. The nave was built in 1851 by the government as a life-saving station. Later owned by Dr. T. Gaillard Thomas who gave it to the congregation. Once called Saint Andrews-By-The-Sea. The Frederic Betts memorial window, *Landscape*, was created in 1906 by Louis Comfort Tiffany.

TAYLOR'S CREEK

An extension of Shinnecock Bay in Southampton. Joseph Taylor (a tailor) is mentioned as a land owner as early as 1708.

TUCKAHOE

A locality west of Southampton Village. The name, according to W.W. Tooker, comes from the Indian word for *Arisaema triphyllum*, commonly called Jack-in-the-Pulpit, a swamp plant whose roots were a source of food.

TUCKAHOE HILL

Within a 135-acre woodland parcel owned privately and by Southampton Town. The hill is 127 feet high. West by North Magee Street, east by Sandy Hollow Road, north by West Neck Road, south by Sebonic Road. Trail entrance is near the Tuckahoe School.

WICKAPOGUE

A district west of Mecox Bay, derived, according to Tooker, from *Weequapaug* and other variants, meaning "at the end of the pond or end of the water."

The first settlers in the locality were Daniel Halsey and his wife Jemima Woodhull in 1688. Wickapogue Road runs east from Old Town Road which is believed to have been the first street in Southampton. Also, Wickapogue Pond.

WINDMILL LANE

In Southampton Village joining North Sea Road. The hilly ground on the west was the site of 18th century windmills. Amagansett has a Windmill Lane which leads north from Main Street. A mill in Setauket (built in 1814) was brought to Abrahams Landing but was destroyed by a fire in 1924.

NORTH SEA

ALEWIFE DREEN

Runs from Big Fresh Pond to North Sea Harbor under Noyac Road. Alewife, a small fish of the herring family, breed in the pond and return to the sea by way of the dreen, an old name for drain, or ditch-like waterway. The word alewife is said to have originated because the fish's fat belly was like those of most women who ran alehouses. A similarly named dreen runs into Morris Cove in Sag Harbor.

BARKERS ISLAND ROAD

William Barker, Southampton's first merchant, built a warehouse on Bullhead Bay at North Sea where he landed goods from sloops. The deed of sale in 1678 describes a parcel "of meadow or island or hummock of meadow lying at Sebonack commonly called the ware-house."

The so-called island is now joined to the swampy mainland by a paved road.

BIG FRESH POND

Actually, a lake—Long Island's second largest—which empties into North Sea Harbor by way of Alewife Creek which runs under Noyac Road.

Alewives swim up this narrow stream to spawn in the fresh water. American eels live in the lake until they swim downstream to Peconic Bay and then over a thousand miles south to the Caribbean Sea. Here they spawn and die and their offspring swim to North America.

BULLHEAD BAY

At North Sea bounded westerly by Sebonic Inlet Road and opening into Little Peconic Bay, called on Beers map (1894) Seabonic Bay. A bullhead is a spiny-headed freshwater fish, also called mud cat and horned pout.

CONSCIENCE POINT

According to tradition, the name originated when, in 1640, the original settlers sailed into the harbor at North Sea and came ashore. A woman said, "For conscience sake, we're on dry land."

The site, a narrow peninsula, is marked by a stone monument dedicated to the colonists from Lynn, Massachusetts, who founded Southampton, the first English settlement in New York State.

The original settlers were Howell, Farrington, Needham, Sayre, Welbe, Walton, Stanborough, Howe, Bread, Cooper, Halsey, Harker, Kyrtland, Newell, Odell and Terry.

Now called Conscience Point National Wildlife Refuge which includes 66 acres of woodland across the water and bounded by North Sea Road. Given to the federal government by Stanley Howard.

COW NECK

A 540-acre peninsula in North Sea bought in 1998 by Louis Bacon, part of the Port of Missing Men and contiguous with Little Peconic Bay, Great Peconic Bay and Scallop Pond. Development rights were donated in 2001 to the Peconic Land Trust. A habitat for many endangered species including piping plovers and ospreys.

DAVIS CREEK

Runs into North Sea Harbor under Towd Point Road. Also called White's Creek after the White family, early 17th century settlers.

EMMA ROSE ELLISTON PARK

Named for Emma Rose Elliston (1856-1933) on what might be the first land (133 acres) granted to Southampton Town for conservation. Located on Millstone Brook Road in North Sea, bounded by Big Fresh Pond. There is a nature trail created by the Southampton Trails Preservation Society.

HERNE STREET

In Little Noyac off Noyac Road in Rose Grove. James A Herne (James A'Herne) 1839-1901, has been called "the American Ibsen", an actor, dramatist, director and stage manager. He wrote many plays; one, *Sag Harbor*, opened in Boston in 1899 and became an overnight smash.

Herne Oaks, Herne's house on his 20-acre retreat on Peconic Bay east of Wooley Pond, was built in 1898 but destroyed by fire in 1909.

HOLMES HILL ROAD

Shown on Beers 1894 map as running northerly from North

Sea Road to Holmes Hill Landing on Little Peconic Bay. No longer in use.

JENNINGS ROAD

In North Sea, linking Scott Road with North Sea Road. In 1668 John Jennings was granted the right to build a fence north of "Noyac River" (the Trout Pond). Elnathan Jennings (1754-1841) was born in Southampton Town and, with his family, left for Connecticut when the British, in 1776, occupied Long Island. As a Continental soldier, he suggested the 1777 commando-like attack on Sag Harbor. This raid, from Guilford, Connecticut, then to Southold and across Peconic Bay, was led by Major Meigs but Sergeant Jennings was the only soldier who knew the area. Twelve British ships were burned and ninety Redcoats were taken prisoner.

MAGUERITE CRABBE GREEFF WILDLIFE SANCTUARY

A ninety-acre portion of the former H. H. Rogers' estate (The Port of Missing Men) near Sebonic Creek at North Sea. Part of Big Woods. Named for the woman who funded the purchase.

MAJOR'S PATH

Possibly named for James White (1746-1801), a major in the

Continental army, this road runs north from Southampton to Noyac Road, east of North Sea Harbor.

MARY'S LANE

Links North Sea Road with Major's Path in North Sea. Named after Mary Haines who lived in a house there in the 18th century.

MILLSTONE BROOK ROAD

A stone, which became one of the early grinding stones for the mill in Water Mill (1644) was taken from a brook in North Sea, out of "the stony brook neere where the mill stone was gotten" (S.H. Town Records, Vol. 6). The brook, which drains from Great Fresh Pond to North Sea Harbor, became known as Mill Stone Brook and gave the name to Millstone Brook Road which runs from North Sea Road to Barker's Island Road. Millstone Lane is off Millstone Brook Road.

MINNESUNK POND

At North Sea. Tooker states that the name was "compounded" in 1866 by George R. Howell, Assistant New York State Librarian. *Minne*, in Siouan meaning water, *sunk* meaning queen. Hence, "Queen of the Waters". Howell might have been describing Big Fresh Pond.

MISSAPOGUE COURT

Off Big Fresh Pond Road in North Sea. Howell suggests that Big Fresh Pond "might appropriately be called Missipaug Lake" but it's not clear that it was ever so named; *Missipaug*, meaning a large body of water.

NORTH SEA

Originally, the port of Southampton, the site of the first landing, in 1640, at Conscience Point by the English families from Lynn, Massachusetts. Granted, in 1650, to John N. Ogden and Company, North Sea Path ran from the harbor to Southampton where there was an Indian settlement. In 1650 a few families were permitted to settle at the harbor. The early name for Peconic Bay to differentiate it from the ocean to the south. At an early time North Sea was called Northampton.

THE PORT OF MISSING MEN

Originally a 1200-acre estate and hunting preserve at North Sea, created by Colonel H. H. Rogers, son of H. H. Rogers (1840-1909), in the early 1900s, encompassing Scallop Pond at Cow Neck and fronting on Little Peconic Bay. His daughter Millicent (1903-1953) was an icon of style. She collected southwest Indian artifacts now housed in the Millicent Rogers Museum in Taos, New Mexico.

The name has at least three possible origins. It could have been the title of a book favored by Rogers. A rudder found on the beach from a ship (*Lykens Valley*) whose crew was lost at sea in 1893 might have suggested the name. Another possibility is that once the gentlemen arrived at the remote shooting preserve they vanished from their wives' purview, control and surveillance.

SCALLOP POND PRESERVE

Off Scott Road in North Sea. A 55-acre wetland preserve of The Nature Conservancy.

SCOTT ROAD

In North Sea, running north from a juncture with Millstone Brook Road to Scallop Pond Road. John Scott, an original settler, built a house there in 1657. Jeckomiah Scott is mentioned as early as 1695 in Pelletreau's Town Records.

SCOTT'S LANDING ROAD

In Towd, near Wooley Pond, running north from Noyac Road to East Beach Road. Named for Lewis Scott or his ancestors, very early settlers.

SPLIT ROCK ROAD

An old woods road south from Great Hill Road in North Sea

and named for a huge glacial erratic. The rock was "split" when it was quarried for material used for the foundation of the Presbyterian church in Southampton Village.

There's also a huge glacial erratic in Montauk's Hither Woods known as Split Rock.

TOWD

The area between Wooley's Pond and North Sea Harbor. Also, a road in Southampton Town, linking Water Mill with North Sea not far from Wooley Pond. The name is, according to Tooker, derived from an Algonquin word meaning a "wading place" perhaps a place on the early path that was a wading place—or two wading places to an island (Towd Island, seen on Beers map of 1894) in what is now Fish Cove. The eastern wading place was filled in and a bridge built around 1875, part of Noyac Road.

TOWD POINT

Reached by Towd Point Road which crosses Davis Creek, once called White's Creek.

TUCKAHOE SWAMP

Water from this area flows into Bullhead Bay. North of White's Lane in North Sea.

WHITE'S LANE

In North Sea linking Barkers Island Road with North Magee Street. White is one of the earliest 17th century Southampton names. This byway may be named for Elias White who lived in the area.

WIRELESS WAY

In North Sea. A residential area close to a facility once owned by International Telephone and Telegraph Company. Close to the Paumanok Path.

WOLF SWAMP LANE

Leads off Big Fresh Pond Road in North Sea, close to 20-acre Wolf Swamp Sanctuary on Big Fresh Pond, a 1957 gift from Elizabeth Morton Tilton. A reminder that before the arrival of Europeans, wolf packs were a keystone species on Long Island and their extermination caused a rise in the deer population. There's a Wolf Way off Red Dirt Road in East Hampton. In 1683, a New York colonial statute awarded a bounty of twenty shillings to anyone killing "a grown wolf on Long Island."

WOOLEY POND

Once named Davis Mill Creek, now a bay in Little Noyac that opens into Little Peconic Bay. Water from Turtle Pond flows into it under Noyac Road and powered a grist mill built around 1692 by John Davis. Pelletreau states that "the Mill Pond is Wooley's Pond." Noyac Road in this area was, on Beers map (1894), called Davis Mill Path. Robert Wooley was an early Southampton settler, who in 1657 owned land at the corner of Post Crossing and Main Street. Wooley Street is in Southampton Village.

WATER MILL

BURNETT CREEK

Close to Flying Point Road and part of Mecox Bay. Thomas Burnett, an original settler of Southampton, had a farm in the area. Burnetts served in the Revolutionary War, World War I, World War II, and Vietnam.

CALF CREEK

In Water Mill. Early maps show that calf pens were located off Mecox Road. The area was originally (1672) called Calf Pen Neck "bounded south and west by Mecox water."

CAMERON BEACH

Alexander Cameron emigrated from Scotland at the turn of the 20th century, the first of a distinguished Southampton family. His son was mayor from 1936 to 1952. W. Scott Cameron Beach is at the west end of Dune Road between the ocean and Mecox Bay.

CAMP POND

Off Deerfield Road in the hills north of Water Mill and south of the Middle Line. In 1737 David Burnett owned "Cap's Pond".

COBB ISLE

In Mecox Bay at the end of Cobb Isle Road. Not quite an isle; connected by a narrow spit to the land. The northern section was donated to the Nature Conservancy. Ospreys, herons, egrets and other species nest here.

COBB ROAD

A district and a road in eastern Southampton, off Montauk Highway. Tooker doubts any aboriginal origin and suggests that the name was associated with cob, or clay, which, when mixed with straw was used for building in the very early days. Also, Cobb Isle Road and Cobb Hill Road.

CORWITH WINDMILL

At the Village Green in Water Mill. Built in 1800 in Sag Harbor and moved in 1813. The name Corwith comes from Carwitham.

FLAX POND

In Water Mill, and one of the seven ponds that feed into Mill Pond. The name could have come from the colonial practice of soaking flax in pond water to prepare it for the extraction of linen fiber used for thread.

FLYING POINT

Mentioned in a 1680 deed concerning the Flying Point Division of lands to be sold by the Proprietors of Southampton.

The ship *Ashland*, sailing from Ireland to Boston in 1846 or 1847, was wrecked here and several hundred were saved.

The name is associated with early off-shore whaling. When a whale was sighted a waft was flown; a waft being an obsolete maritime word for a signal flag.

FORDUNE DRIVE

Off Wickapogue Drive in Water Mill. The name is derived from Henry Ford II who owned a mansion and over two hundred acres with a quarter of a mile of ocean front.

LUTHER DRIVE

Could be named for an early settler, Luther Burnett.

MECOX DUNE PRESERVE

On Dune Road fronting on Mecox Bay and a smaller section on the ocean. A valuable holding of the Nature Conservancy but unfortunately overgrown with *Phragmites communis*.

MILL POND LANE

In Water Mill, named for the pond *(Nowedonah)* that was the source of power for Edward Howell's original watermill, built in 1644. Water empties into Mill Creek.

MORRISON LANE

South of the highway in Water Mill, off Bay Lane, close to the water of Mecox Bay. Names for John Morrison (1929-2004) who owned acreage in the vicinity.

NOWEDONAH LANE

A sachem of the Shinnecock Indians who, with three other chiefs, signed the original deed for the Town of Southampton. Nowedonah Lane in Water Mill leads off of Route 27. Mill Pond, in Water Mill, is also known as Lake Nowedonah and covers 85 acres. Tooker tells us that the name in

Algonquin means "the seeker." His home was at North Sea near Conscience Point.

OLD MILL ROAD

Connects the Montauk Highway—originally called The Mill Path—with Head of the Pond Road. The functioning mill here isn't the 1644 mill of Edward Howell but is close to the first site. The settlers built a mill dam to contain the water of Mill Pond and cut an opening (a gut) from Mecox Bay to the ocean to lower the level for the water-wheel. The mill created a small community and eventually took the name Water Mill.

PROPRIETORS LANE

In Water Mill running from the Montauk Highway to Halsey Lane; this area was originally owned by the first proprietors in the original (1640) grant of land, most of which became common grazing land. The adjacent cemetery was once part of this land as was the Corwith Windmill.

ROSEMARY LODGE

In Water Mill at 322 Rose Hill Road and in the National Register of Historic Places. Built in 1884 by Henry Turbell Rose, a Presbyterian minister and a summer minister in Bridgehampton who died in 1919. He was a descendant of the very old and distinguished Rose family. Mrs. Rose's name was Mary, hence the name.

SAYRE'S POND

There's a Sayre's Pond in Water Mill, one of the Seven Ponds. There's another Sayre's Pond in Wickapogue just east of Fowler Street on the way to the beach. Sayre is an original (1640) settler name.

SEVEN PONDS

In Water Mill, the seven ponds close to Lake Nowedonah (Mill Pond) and the 1644 mill: Sayre Pond, Gideon Pond (Gideon Halsey), Flax Pond, Cow Pond, Darby's Pond and Callahan's Pond (later called Malone's Swamp). A seventh pond is unnamed.

STATION ROAD

In Water Mill and named for the second station of the Long Island Railroad built in 1903 and closed in 1933. The original station was built in 1875. Local fish and potatoes were shipped from here.

STEVEN HALSEY'S PATH

Off Cobb Road in the Downe's Farm subdivision. Since 1640 there have been several Steven Halseys on the South Fork; this road was named by Charlton Halsey after his great-grandfather, born in 1818, who died in 1875.

SWAN CREEK

In Mecox, an estuary that flows into Mecox Bay. Most likely named, not for the majestic bird, but for J.A. Swan, a pastor of the First Methodist Church which was built in 1820.

VILLA OF SAINT JOSEPH

On Rose Hill Road in Water Mill. Built in 1893 as an inn, it was bought by the Catholic Church and renamed as a retreat for seminarians. Used to house troops during World War II, it became a retreat and vacation center for the Sisters of Mercy.

VILLA MARIA

Formerly a Dominican convent in Water Mill between Halsey Lane and Mill Creek called the Siena Spirituality Center, named for Catherine of Siena (1347-1380), a Catholic saint known for her revelations and responsible for Pope Gregory XI's return from Avignon to Rome. Built in 1887 and altered by its various owners.

WATER MILL

The original hamlet took its name from a water-mill built in 1644 by Edward Howell who was granted forty acres and the right to build a dam between Seven Ponds and Mecox Bay and construct a mill.

Mill Road was the name of the original road, now Montauk Highway, that ran eastward from the original (1640) settlement at Southampton to the mill.

The octagon-shaped windmill, restored in 1987, was first used by James Carwitham in 1814 after it had been moved from North Haven. The name Carwitham—with origins in Cornwall—was changed to Corwith.

WATER MILL BEACH CLUB

The original clubhouse, built in 1922 at Flying Point, was destroyed in the Hurricane of 1938. The present club was built the following year close to the ocean beach that was once a site of off-shore whaling.

WATER MILL COMMUNITY HOUSE

On Main Street in Water Mill. Designed by architect Walter E. Brady as a chapel in 1898. The building was never used by any particular church but as a meeting hall for various community groups.

SAG HARBOR AND NOYAC

ACKERLY STREET

In Sag Harbor, off Clinton Street. Robert Ackerly lived in Southold in 1651, the ancestor of an old and distinguished Long Island family. Pelletreau states that "George and Robert Ackerly were soldiers in Sag Harbor in 1813." Perhaps they or other members of the family settled there.

AMERICAN HOTEL

On Main Street in Sag Harbor, built around 1845 by Nathan

Tinker in the Gothic Revival style. A former inn on the site, James Howell's, was the British headquarters during the Revolutionary War. Officers here were taken prisoner in 1777 by American raiders under Jonathan Meigs and taken to Connecticut.

The American Hotel, Sag Harbor

ANNA AND DANIEL MULVIHILL PRESERVE

Purchased in 2001 by Southampton Town to preserve groundwater and varied habitats for flora and fauna. This 75-acre preserve is named for D.F. Mulvihill (1883-1968) and his wife Anna McDonough (1897-1964) who bought the land in the 1920s. In the Great Swamp area between Brickiln Road and Scuttlehole Road.

*Wetlands in The Anna and Daniel Mulvihill Preserve
Habitat for a vast abundance of species*

ANNIE COOPER BOYD HOUSE

On Sag Harbor's Main Street and owned by the Sag Harbor Historical Society. Also called the Herald House, it was built in the 18th century. Annie Cooper Boyd's daughter was Nancy Boyd Willey who died in 1998.

AZUREST

A community off Hampton Street in Sag Harbor, created in 1947 by Maude Meredith Terry (1887-1968) and named for the color of the water of Gardiners Bay. She also named some streets to remember her relations (Terry Drive, Meredith Avenue) and to remember "the heritage of Afro-Americans and Indians in Sag Harbor."

BRICKILN ROAD

The name appears on maps noting that it existed as early as 1690. Clay deposits on land more recently owned by William White, then the Collins family and later D.F. Mulvihill, led to the creation of a brick-making establishment and, consequently, the name. The meandering road leads from Sag Harbor to a junction with Scuttlehole Road.

Another road, leading into the area from the Bridgehampton Sag Harbor Turnpike is called Claypit Road. Farther south on the Turnpike there was a brickyard. Open clay pits, some of them now ponds, and evidences of brick-making may be found in these areas. Jeannette Rattray notes that Josiah Hand (1756-1835) lived "at the Brick Kilns between Sag Harbor and Bridgehampton."

BURKE STREET

Off Bay Street in Sag Harbor, named for Michael Burke who arrived in 1820, became a Catholic leader and was responsible for the first Catholic Church in the village. Lieutenant John Wallace Burke was an officer in the 81st New York Volunteer Regiment, was killed in 1864 at Cold Harbor and is buried in Oakland Cemetery.

BURKSHIRE PLACE

South off Noyac Road in Noyac and named by the owner Edward O Burke.

CADMUS DRIVE

At Azurest, in Sag Harbor, named after the whaleship *Cadmus*, owned by Cornelius Sleight, that in 1824, brought back to America the French general Lafayette who had served with George Washington in the Revolution. David Hand, Jr. of Sag Harbor was, in 1836, the whaling master. The *Cadmus* made fifteen voyages and in 1849 sailed to California, where, deemed unfit for further sailing, she became a storeship. Cadmus, in Greek mythology, was the builder of Thebes.

CHATFIELD'S HILL

In Sag Harbor, named for Thomas Chatfield (1609-1687) or his descendants. The Chatfield family was one of the original settlers of East Hampton and presumed to have been descended from landed gentry in England. Also, Chatfield's Creek, in Springs.

CHRIST EPISCOPAL CHURCH

Three Tiffany windows, a brass pulpit and a marble altar adorn this house of worship on Sag Harbor's Division Street.

CHURCH STREET

In Sag Harbor. Named for an 18th century building standing where Church Street crosses Sage Street. Once called the "Old Barn" church and also the "Old Brown Meeting House". It was originally a Presbyterian church but was demolished.

The second church was sold to the Episcopal Church and later moved to the northwest corner of Church and Union Streets. It then became the "Atheneum" which burned down in 1924.

CIVIL WAR MONUMENT

Company K of the 127th New York Volunteer Infantry Regiment was recruited in Sag Harbor, fought in many actions and occupied Charleston, South Carolina at the war's end. The regiment was called "The Clamdiggers" because of their zeal for digging for clams on the barrier islands of Georgia. Many Sag Harbor men—John Wallace Burke and Peter French—joined the 81st New York (the colonel was Edwin Rose, a local man) and other units of the army and navy.

A granite statue of a Union Soldier stands at the intersection of Main Street and Madison Avenue.

CLAM ISLAND

In Noyac Bay east of Jessup's Neck. Mentioned in 1689 in a sale by Jeckomiah Scott, "Meadowland...and a place called Clam Island". Not a true island; connected to the mainland by a narrow spit. Once owned by the Tredwell family. Since 1988, a 20-acre Suffolk County park and wildlife sanctuary. Ospreys nest here.

CLINTON STREET

In Sag Harbor. George Clinton (1739-1812) was the first

Civil War Monument, Sag Harbor

popularly elected governor of New York and a most important leader during the Revolutionary War. Re-elected six times, he died as James Madison's vice president.

CLONMOYLAN WOODS

Named by the author for the townland in Co. Galway, Ireland where Patrick Mulvihill, the author's grandfather, was born in 1846. He served in the Civil War, settled in Connecticut, became a hatter and had 13 children. Over ten acres, between Bridgehampton and Sag Harbor off Clay Pit Road. Purchased by Suffolk County for open space in 2009. The Anna and Daniel Mulvihill Preserve connects Clonmoylan Woods to The William Mulvihill Preserve.

CONKLING'S POINT

The waterfront area in Sag Harbor where, in later years, the breakwater was built. Joseph Conkling (1709-1792) with John Foster (born around 1720), delegate to the first Provincial Congress of 1775, owned ships. Joseph's son, Joseph Stratton Conkling, was captain of a privateer in the Revolution symbolically named *Revenge*. Another son, Edward (1745-1779) was a privateer, captain of *Beaver* and *Eagle*. The family had joined the exodus of local people to Connecticut. A very old family which came to East Hampton in 1650 and produced many distinguished men and women. Alfred Conkling (1789-1874) born in Amagansett, was a Congressman and in 1852, Minister to Mexico.

COOPER STREET

An 18th century road in Sag Harbor that ran from Main Street to the wharf. Named for Caleb Cooper (1751-1840), this street is now extinct. James Fenimore Cooper, the novelist, was part-owner, in 1819, of the whale ship *Union*. Born in New Jersey, he was related to the Long Island Coopers. His wife's cousin, Mrs. Charles T. Dering, lived in Sag Harbor. East Hampton's Cooper Lane links Newtown Lane with Cedar Street.

CROSS STREET

At one time this Sag Harbor street was called Leonard Street after James Leonard, a town trustee around 1850.

CUFFEE DRIVE

Off Bay Street in Sag Harbor. Paul Cuffee (1757-1812) was an Indian minister, a "Shinecoc." Lewis Cuffee, descended from blacks and Shinnecock Indians, organized in 1840 a group of blacks and created the A.M.E. Zion Church in Eastville, Sag Harbor. Other members were Charles Plato of East Hampton and William Prime of Sag Harbor, named as the first trustees.

Warren Cuffee, a Civil War veteran, died with 28 others attempting to re-float the *Circassian* which was stranded on a bar off Mecox on December 29, 1876. He's buried at the Shinnecock Reservation.

Custom House, Sag Harbor

CUSTOM HOUSE

Built in 1789, the first custom house in the state and Long Island's first post office. Originally at Union and Church Street, the home of Yale-educated Henry Packer Dering (1763-1822) was moved to Garden Street. Sag Harbor was designated an official Port of Entry in 1789 by the first U.S. Congress and collected federal duties on imported goods and on ships. In those early years, Sag Harbor was a busier port than New York City.

The house, open to the public, is furnished with over 3,000 objects including decorative arts and crafts.

DAYTON'S BAY

A former name of Sag Harbor Cove. Also, Dayton's Pond.

John Jermain had a channel dug from the cove to the Otter Pond. In 1955, novelist John Steinbeck left California and bought a house fronting on "the cove." Dayton's Island is in the channel at Three Mile Harbor in East Hampton.

Dayton is one of the oldest and most distinguished family names on the South Fork. The original ancestor was born in 1588 in England and died in East Hampton in 1658. Daniel Dayton was a captain in the War of 1812. Charles Bolivar Dayton was a surgeon in the 127th New York Volunteer Regiment. Wounded in action, he survived to become a doctor in East Hampton and lived in the "1770 House."

DERING ROAD

Thomas Dering (1720-1785) was one of the early settlers of Shelter Island, hence Dering Harbor. Also a Sag Harbor road leading in to Bay Street.

Henry Packer Dering was the first United States postmaster on Long Island and was appointed in 1794 by Thomas Pickering. Dering was also Federal Agent and Collector of Port. He died in 1822 while in office. C.T. Dering was an owner of whale ships in the 19th century, among them the *Sabrina*. N.R. Dering was the master of *Mary Ann* (1842) and never returned from a sea voyage.

DIVISION STREET

The street in Sag Harbor which divides the village into

Southampton Town and East Hampton Town. The Division Line was created in 1695 by an agreement between an East Hampton group and a committee chosen to represent Southampton. The two towns agreed to lay out a highway one rod in width on either side of the line. The East Hampton Group consisted of a Hobart, a Dayton, a Wheeler, a Conkling, a Mulford and a Hand. Family names from Southampton included Howell, Pierson, Topping, Cooper, and Cook.

DODSON'S POND

In Sag Harbor, across from Pierson High School, once a pond, then a dump and, in 1975, covered over by a bulldozer.

DUKE FORDHAM'S INN

No longer existing. It was on the west wide of Sag Harbor's Main Street. Here, James Fenimore Cooper wrote his first novel, *Precaution*.

EASTVILLE AVENUE

Named for Eastville, an area in Sag Harbor, originally settled by freed slaves, and some runaway slaves. Eastville was originally named Snooksville after an English family named Snooks who were there in the early 1700s. A number of Eastville men found employment in the whaling trade. In the 1800s, members of Eastville (David Hempstead, Lewis Cuffee, Charles Plato, William Prime) created St. David's African Methodist Episcopal Church, located on the avenue.

FORE AND AFT

A small pond close to Round Pond and Long Pond which is described in nautical terms, due, most likely, because of the proximity of Sag Harbor with its long maritime tradition.

FOSTER BEACH

At Noyac, a public beach on Peconic Bay owned, in 1950, by Charles H. Foster and Everett C. Foster. Foster is an ancient local name. John Foster, born around 1720, was a delegate to the First Provincial Congress of 1755.

FROGLAND

Wetlands behind the Mulvihill homestead in what is now The Anna and Daniel Mulvihill Preserve. Home to a great abundance of wildlife.

GENISSEE SWAMP

On a 1916 map of Sag Harbor, a Genissee Creek emanates from a swamp south of Jermain Avenue and flows into the Otter Pond, through land owned by C.N. Archibald. The "creek" no longer exists but the swamp has survived.

W.W. Tooker tells us that the name is derived from the Onondaga Indian language, *gennis-he-yo* meaning "the beautiful valley." The Genissee Valley in western New York State, in the early 1800s was known for the beauty and richness of its land.

GLOVER STREET

Named after Benjamin Glover whose fifteen-room, Federal style, shingled house stands on the north corner of the street, fronting on Main Street. Glover was a carpenter-builder and cabinetmaker. The Glover house was built around 1820.

Alfred C. Glover, master of the whaleship *Acasta*, died at sea in 1836, one of five captains remembered on the Broken Mast Monument in Sag Harbor's Oakland Cemetery. He was 29.

The author of this book was born in the old McDonough homestead on Glover Street.

GREAT SWAMP

A fifteen-acre drained kettlehole bog and surrounding acreage lying between Scuttlehole Road and Brickiln Road. One of the many Long Island bogs left by the retreating glacier some fifteen thousand years ago. This area is covered with Swamp Maple (*Acer rubrum*), American fern and mixed oak, beech and pine forest. A rich diversity of flowering plants thrive there, some very rare. A haven for dozens of bird species, including nesting migratory songbirds as well as countless mammal, reptile and insect species. Its vernal ponds are a sanctuary for a wide variety of amphibians.

Humus in Great Swamp has a depth of over twenty feet. Great Swamp Dreen runs east, under the Bridgehampton Sag

Harbor Turnpike carrying water to the Long Pond Greenbelt. Located on the groundwater divide of the South Fork, Great Swamp and the surrounding wetlands are a critical groundwater recharge area and an important drinking water resource for the future.

Now part of The William Mulvihill Preserve created in 2006 following the author's death in 2004.

GREEN STREET

Off Glover Street in Sag Harbor. The waterfront area here was once called Peter's Green, after Peter Hildreth. A shipyard built ocean-going sailing ships, such as the small schooner *San Diego* that Jared Wade (1811-1889) sailed to California during the Gold Rush.

Another industry was the L'Hommedieu rope-manufacturing business and Peter Hildreth's windmill.

HANNIBAL FRENCH HOUSE

Built in 1792 and added to by renowned architect Minard Lafever in 1834. Hannibal French owned several whaling ships. The house is on lower Main Street in Sag Harbor.

HARRY'S LANE

Off Noyac Road at Pine Neck and named for H.H. Treadwell

who died in 1950, a descendant of a settler family of the 1600s. Built by Henry Hewlett Treadwell, Jr. in 1957.

HAVENS BEACH

A public beach (Havens Memorial Park) at Sag Harbor, also known as Tighe's Beach, named for Judge James G. Tighe and then for Frank Coulton Havens (1846-1916) whose mansion was just west of the present beach. The beach was sold to Sag Harbor by Lila Havens, Frank's second wife. Havens, the uncle of the poet George Sterling, made his fortune in San Francisco. The Havens mansion is now Cormaria Retreat House, an interfaith sanctuary run by the Catholic community, the Religious of the Sacred Heart of Mary.

Havens is an old and distinguished Shelter Island—Sag Harbor name. Jacob Havens was first mate on the whale ship *Manhattan*, which in 1845—eight years prior to Commodore Perry's visit—entered a Tokyo bay to return shipwrecked sailors to the anti-foreign, self-isolated shogun. One of the original settlers of North Haven was Jonathan Havens, a doctor and prominent landholder. Frank Haven's father was Wickham Havens, a whaling captain. Frank's nephew was George Ansel Sterling (1869-1926), born in Sag Harbor, who went to San Francisco and became a well-known poet, friend of Jack London and Ambrose Bierce.

HEMPSTEAD STREET

David Hempstead was a leader of the Black community in Eastville (Sag Harbor) in the late 1800s. Hempstead was instrumental in the establishment of the African Methodist Society and the creation in 1863 of St. David's African Methodist Episcopal Zion Church. David Hempstead died in 1886 and is buried in the church cemetery on Eastville Avenue, as are Civil War veterans Charles Prime, Charles Dipp, Charles Green, James Van Houten, Joseph Prince and Simon Hasbrook.

HERALD HOUSE

On Main Street in Sag Harbor. Once owned by preservationist Nancy Boyd Willey (1902-1998), the house (1735) was bequeathed to the Sag Harbor Historical Society. Also known as the Annie Cooper Boyd House (the mother of Nancy Boyd Willey).

Called, in error, The Herald House. David Frothingham's newspaper, *The Long Island Herald*, established in 1791 was printed in a house across the street which no longer exists.

HOPPY TOAD HILL

Highest point of land in The Anna and Daniel Mulvihill Preserve. Also known as The Cathedral by hikers, it is covered with a white pine forest planted by the author, his wife and his parents in the early twentieth century. Important nesting area for numerous species.

JERMAIN AVENUE

Named in memory of John Jermain (1758-1819), the grandfather of Mrs. Russell Sage, whose generosity resulted in the John Jermain Library in 1910, Mashashimuet Park, Pierson High School (her mother's name), the Noyac Chapel and the Otter Pond. She also created the Russell Sage Foundation, a charitable organization based in Manhattan. Russell Sage died in 1906 and left his wife $65,000,000.

John Jermain served as a major in the War of 1812 as commander of a fort in Sag Harbor. His grandson, Joseph Jermain Slocum, was a colonel in the Civil War. The long twisting road connects Main Street with Division Street.

JESSE HALSEY LANE

Off Brickiln Road in Sag Harbor, named for Jesse R. Halsey (1806-1898) who was in the West Indian trade and became a whaler.

JESSUP'S NECK

Once called Farrington's Neck after the original 1640 settlers John and Thomas Farrington. Granted to John Jessup in 1679 "the point called Noyack" by the Southampton Town Proprietors as his lot in a 40-acre division of land.

Now called The Elizabeth A. Morton National Wildlife Refuge after Elizabeth Morton who, in 1954, donated the 189 acres to the federal government. A nesting site for the roseate tern, least tern, osprey and piping plover.

JOEL LANE

Off Jermain Avenue in Sag Harbor and running to Round Pond. Named for Joseph (Joe) Labrozzi (L), a local builder.

JOHN JERMAIN LIBRARY

In 1910, a gift to Sag Harbor by Mrs. Russell Sage and a memorial to her grandfather John Jermain. Her grandmother was Margaret Pierson whom she remembered by the gift of the local public school. Designed by Augustus Allen, the library is in the Classical Revival Style and in the National Register of Historic Places.

JOHN JERMAIN'S MILL

Once (around 1793) located close to a stream that ran into Sag Harbor's Otter Pond.

LAMB'S CORNER

Where Brickiln Road begins at the Bridgehampton Sag Harbor Turnpike (Main Street). Most likely named for Joseph P. Lamb who, in 1842, built the local Presbyterian Church.

LATHAM STREET

Off Division Street in Sag Harbor and named after an early settler, possibly Elijah Latham. Roy Latham (1881-1979) of Orient was Long Island's most gifted, self-taught naturalist whose collections and prolific writings on botany and entomology form the basis for much of Long Island ecological studies. The site of Pierson High School was once called Latham's Hill.

LIGONEE

A swamp and a brook at Sag Harbor flowing from 75-acre Long Pond into the Cove, forming the southwestern boundary of the village. Also known as the Alewife Drain or Elwhy Dreen—a dreen being an East End term for drain or ditch. Alewife is a fish.

The root of the word, according to Tooker, is not Indian; rather taken from an incident where a man sank into the swamp "Leg an' knee."

LITTLE NOYAC

Once used to designate the land between Jessup's Neck and Wooley Pond (Davis Mill Creek) and mentioned as early as 1702 in a deed of a sale of "a mill and a mill house" to Jonathan Davis.

Long Pond near head of Ligonee Creek
Very important ecological area in Sag Harbor

LONG POND GREENBELT

A 1000-plus acre preserve of forest, swamps and ponds stretching southward from Sag Harbor's Otter Pond to Sagg Pond in Sagaponack. Created by various conservation groups and local governments.

LONG WHARF

The original authorization to build a 35-foot wide wharf at Sagg Harbor was given in 1770 to a wharf company subscribed by a group of local men. This historic structure played a role in the Revolutionary War (when it was one of the objectives of the Meigs Raid), the War of 1812, the era of whaleships and the sea-bourne commerce that made Sag Harbor a renowned port.

LOPER'S PATH

Off Old Sag Harbor Road in Purgatory. One of the original settler families of East Hampton; the Lopers were Dutch. Jacob Loper, the first of the illustrious family, was captain of a Dutch man-of-war and in 1646 sat on the Council of New Amsterdam (New York).

James Loper was a famous offshore whaler and West Indies trader in the 17th century. Jeanette Rattray in her *Up and Down Mainstreet* says that a Pacific island is named for him. At one point in his varied life he was invited to Nantucket to educate the inhabitants about "the techniques of whale fishing."

Abram Benjamin Loper served in Company K, 127th N.Y. Volunteers during the Civil War and died at Morris Island, South Carolina. Henry Loper of the 81st New York was killed at Cold Harbor in 1864.

LOVE LANE

A narrow road between Division Street and Rysam Street in Sag Harbor. According to one source, there was once a lane here running through a meadow. A swing was suspended from a rope tied to two large trees on either side of the lane. The swing became "a trysting place" for young couples, hence the name.

MANKESACK ISLAND

Everett Rattray, who spelled it Manhansack, wrote that the island "disappeared long ago." Pelletreau notes that in 1712, Sacatoco, an Indian "of Montocket" sold to Robert Cody "all that island lying and being in the Sound or Harbor between Hog Neck (North Haven) and Sag Harbor or thereabouts called by the name of Mankesack or Stony Island and all that can be found unpatented in the bounds of East Hampton from the north side of Alewife Brook Neck."

MASHASHIMUET PARK

Named, according to Tooker, for the springs on the south side of the Otter Pond. The word, in Algonkin, means "at the great spring." In the 19th century, there were heaps of shells in the locality, as well as Indian graves and relics. Mrs. Russell Sage, on the advice of William Wallace Tooker, used the Indian name. Included in the 60-acre park is the Otter Pond and the springs that attracted the Indians. Samuel Parsons, a landscape architect, designed the park. In 1920 the Russell Sage Foundation deeded the park to the Park and Recreation Association of Sag Harbor. It's managed by an independent park board.

MEADOWLARK LANE

In Sag Harbor running off Main Street. An early name for Sag Harbor was Great Meadow because of the low land–occasionally flooded–west of Main Street. The original name could have been Meadow Lane.

METHODIST HILL

In Sag Harbor at the top of High Street, also called Fort Hill or Sleight's Hill. The original Methodist Church (1811) stood here until it was moved (1835) to Madison Street.

MIDDLE LINE HIGHWAY

A short road in eastern Sag Harbor that takes its name from "the middle line", a surveyor's base line created in 1739 which forms the Great North and South Division on the South Fork. The "middle line," not a highway, forms the boundary of hundreds of parcels of real estate.

MILL CREEK

Once called Ruggs Creek. In Noyac at Pine Neck with a narrow channel leading to Noyac Bay. Named for an ancient water-mill powered by water running from the Trout Pond into the creek.

MILLSTONE ROAD

Runs north from Scuttlehole Road to Noyac, named because a stone from a swamp "at Scuttlehole" was fashioned into a grinding stone for the mill at Water Mill.

MORRIS COVE

An arm of the Sag Harbor Cove reaching south close to Noyac Road. Fed by Ligonee Creek (the Alewife Drain). The name's origin is unknown.

MOTT'S POND

Now filled in and generally the site of the American Legion building in Sag Harbor on Bay Street. The first Mott to arrive in Sag Harbor was Captain Henry Mott (1796-1849) from Northport, a descendant of William Mott (1712-1818). The name was originally French, de la Mott.

MOUNT MISERY ROAD

Off Madison Avenue in Sag Harbor. One theory of the name's origin is that in times past, poor or needy people went to the house of a good Samaritan here for food and assistance.

MULFORD LANE

Off Bay Street in Sag Harbor. Mulford is an old and distinguished name. John and William Mulford were among

Along the Mulvihill Loop Trail, up on Hoppy Toad Hill

the early settlers. Colonel David Mulford of East Hampton raised a regiment during the Revolutionary War. Mulford and Sleight formed a company which owned sailing ships at the port of Sag Harbor in the 1840s. Also, Mulford Avenue off Old Northwest Path, Mulford Lane in Napeague, Mulford Avenue off Flamingo Avenue in Montauk.

MULVIHILL POND

A spring-fed pond north of Great Swamp (north of Scuttlehole Road) named for D.F. Mulvihill (1883-1968) who once owned the pond and the surrounding woodland. Now part of the 75-acre Anna (1897-1964) and Daniel Mulvihill Preserve. Important to many migratory birds.

MUNCHOGUE DRIVE

South of Mill Creek in Pine Neck at Noyac. William Wallace Tooker claimed that the Algonkin word *Munchoag* (many spellings) was associated with "rushes" or "an island of rushes." Rushes were salt marsh grasses used by Indians and mowed by early settlers for fodder.

Star Island in Lake Montauk was originally called Munchog.

MUNICIPAL BUILDING

On Sag Harbor's Main Street, built in 1846 by Ezekiel Mulford. Once the Mansion Hotel, owned by the Mulford family (Prentice Mulford). Later became the Union School.

NANCY BOYD WILLEY PARK

A small, crescent-shaped piece of land on the east side of the Bridgehampton Sag Harbor Turnpike close to the southern border of Sag Harbor. Named in 1996 for Nancy Willey (1902-1998) a founding member of the Old Sag Harbor Committee, an environmentalist who initiated the Long Pond Greenbelt, an historian and preservationist.

NINEVEH BEACH

Fronting on Gardiner's Bay west of Little Northwest Creek in Sag Harbor. Harry Sleight suggests that because "a bawdy crowd" lived near the beach in early times, it took the name Nineveh from "the wicked city" of antiquity, the capital of Assyria that Jonah wanted God to destroy. Now an upscale residential area.

NORTHAMPTON COLONY

Built by Henry Hewlett Treadwell, Sr. in the 1930s. Off Noyac Road and contiguous with the Elizabeth A. Morton National Wildlife Refuge (Jessup's Neck).

NOYAC

A bay, a creek, a road and a locality close to Sag Harbor (also spelled Noyack) named from an Indian word meaning a long neck of land (Jessup's Neck).

In May, 1777, Colonel Meigs left Connecticut with 130 men in 13 whaleboats and came ashore at Noyac Bay. Led by a Southampton Town native Elnathan Jennings they marched at night down Brickiln Road (note monument) to British occupied Sag Harbor and surprised the sleeping garrison, taking 90 prisoners, mostly Loyalists, and burning several ships.

OLD BURYING GROUND

In Sag Harbor at Union and Madison Streets, next to the Presbyterian Church, opened in 1767. The first interment was James Howell. One grave is that of William Havens who fought in the Revolution as a privateer, commanding the *Jay, Beaver* and *Retaliation*. Sixteen other veterans of the Revolution are buried here as well as a representative to the first Provincial Congress in 1775.

A monument (1902) reads:

> *A British fort near this spot was captured by the Americans under Lieut. Colonel Meigs at the Battle of Sag Harbor, May 23, 1777.*

Also presumed to be buried here are four Loyalist soldiers killed during the fight for the fort.

OTTER HOSE COMPANY

The first volunteer fire fighting company in New York State was formed in Sag Harbor in 1819 after a disastrous fire in 1817 spread to warehouses filled with whale oil. Some twenty stores and homes were destroyed. The fire house on Main Street, faces the Otter Pond.

OTTER POND

Originally a fresh water pond and the habitat of the river otter, now close to extinction on Long Island. John Jermain, in 1783, had a channel dug to the cove "so that fish may not be hindered from coming in." The brackish pond, bought by Mrs. Russell Sage in 1911, became part of Mashashimuet Park.

PALMER TERRACE

Runs from Sag Harbor's Main Street to Jermain Avenue; a residential area created and named for Francis Palmer around 1895.

PAYNE'S CREEK

Part of Sag Harbor Cove. At one time called Staff Pain's Creek (according to Sleight). There was a family named Pain in North Haven and in Little Noyac. The name could also be derived from Payne, an early and distinguished South Fork name.

Charles W. Payne, master of the whale ship *Fanny* died at

sea in 1838 at age 30 and is remembered on the Broken Mast Monument in Sag Harbor's Oakland Cemetery. John Howard Payne, son of William, author of *Home Sweet Home*, was born in 1791 in an East Hampton house that is now a museum. He was the first (1842-1845) American diplomat to represent his country in Tunis.

PIERSON HIGH SCHOOL

Abraham Pierson (Cambridge, 1632) was a founder of Southampton and its first minister. He signed the original Indian deed in 1640 and remained as minister until 1647. William Pierson of Bridgehampton was master of the brig *American* and remembered on the Broken Mast Monument in Sag Harbor's Oakland Cemetery. He died in 1836 at 30 on a whaling venture in the Pacific. Mrs. Russell Sage's mother was a Pierson, and Sag Harbor's public high school, built with Sage money, was named Pierson High School, completed in 1907.

PURGATORY

Also, Purgatory Hollow, described by Ernest Clowes as "the deep and dark hollow in the hills north of the first crest of hills and westward of the Brickiln Road". Named, no doubt, for the region between Heaven and Hell. Here, it was said, cattle were hidden by colonial farmers during the Revolutionary War to protect them from confiscation by the occupying British regulars and from foraging Loyalist soldiers under the overall command of Colonel Oliver DeLancey.

The Broken Mast Monument in Oakland Cemetery, Sag Harbor Dedicated to Captain John Howell and to Southampton Town whaling captains killed during the pursuit of whales

RECTOR STREET

William Lawrence was, from 1865-66, a pastor (rector) of the Methodist Church who lived on this street and the name might be derived from this fact. The street connects Division Street with Bay Street in Sag Harbor.

REDWOOD

The name of the 70-acre peninsula called, in early days, Brushy Neck, perhaps an island at one time, at the end of Glover Street in Sag Harbor. Owned, in 1818, by Benjamin Glover.

The name was once "Woodruffs" after John Woodruff who owned this land in 1860. Later known as Morton's Neck (around 1875) after another owner, Dr. William J. Morton of New York City who sold it in 1924.

ROGERS STREET

Links Latham Street with Henry Street in Sag Harbor. Rogers is an old South Fork name. John Rogers, a captain during the Civil War, was Street Commissioner of Sag Harbor and perhaps this is the derivation of the name.

ROSE STREET

In Sag Harbor, named for Colonel Abram Rose, a Bridgehampton military officer who during the War of 1812 raised volunteers, many from Sag Harbor.

We assume that Rose Grove, in North Sea, and Rose Grove Road were named after Robert Rose, one of the early Southampton settlers. Edwin Rose (1807-1864), a graduate of West Point, raised the 81st New York Volunteer Infantry Regiment and served as its colonel in the Civil War. When he resigned, Lincoln appointed him Provost Marshal of Long Island. Deerfield Road was once called The Road to Rose Grove. Also Rose Hill Road in Water Mill running from the Montauk Highway to Mecox Bay.

RUGGS PATH

Also a neck and a creek at Noyac. Ruggs Stream is (according to Tooker) the brook that runs from "Thompson's Trout Pond". Ruggs Path runs from Noyac Road to Millstone Road. Ruggs are buried in the North Sea Cemetery on Millstone Brook Road.

RUM HILL

A Sag Harbor neighborhood around Madison Street and Elizabeth Street. A fanciful rumor has it that a local sailor, who died at sea, was brought back to port in a barrel of whiskey so that his wish to be buried in Sag Harbor might be realized.

RYSAM STREET

In Sag Harbor, off Bay Street. Captain William Johnson Rysam (1737-1809) of Sag Harbor "owned and built ships for the West Indian trade and had a mahogany grove in

Honduras." He was also a large landowner, the father of five daughters and created a fund to educate poor children. His second wife was Phebe Mulford of East Hampton.

The captain's son-in-law was Cornelius Sleight. The two men built ships and were involved in other commercial enterprises.

SAG HARBOR

Early English settlers on the South Fork discovered that a mainstay of the Indian diet was a tuber that grew in abundance in low swampy areas. This edible tuber has many names: groundnut, Indian potato, wild bean, bog potato; its scientific name is *Apios tuberosa*. The original Pilgrims ate them during their first precarious New England winter and botanists believe it to be one of the most important of wild foods and, had it not been for the potato, the groundnut would have been the first tuber to be cultivated.

The Indians called the plant sagga and the word found its way into *Saggabon, Sagabonak, Sagg*. The harbor of Sagg evolved into Sag Harbor, which was also once known as Great Meadows.

SAG HARBOR WHALING MUSEUM

The imposing building opposite the library on Main Street. Built in 1845 by Benjamin Huntting II it was, in 1907, bought by Margaret Slocum Sage (1828-1918), wife of Russell Sage

(1815-1906). This building was probably designed by renowned architect Minard Lafever who created the Old Whalers' Church.

SAG HARBOR YACHT CLUB

Created in 1897 and relocated to its present site in 1912 on property given by Frank C. Havens, who was instrumental in the creation of the breakwater in 1908 which protects the yacht club boats and other vessels.

SAGE STREET

In Sag Harbor, off Madison Street which in early days was called Meeting-House Hill. Dr. Ebenezer Sage (1755-1834) graduated from Yale in 1788 and settled in East Hampton. He was, for three terms, a member of Congress (1809-1817). Sage is a modification of La Sarge and the early ancestors were French Huguenots. He was buried in the Old Burying Ground, then reinterred in Oakland Cemetery.

Ebenezer's son John Smith Sage (1791-1882) graduated from Dartmouth and became a doctor in Sag Harbor. He never married and in his later years became a recluse.

SAGG ROAD

The oldest road in Sag Harbor leading in from Sagaponack. The northern end in Sag Harbor is Madison Street, named for the President.

SAINT ANDREW'S SCHOOL

The first (1860) Catholic school on Long Island. Now demolished but replaced by the Stella Maris School. The school was created by the Religious of the Sacred Heart, an order founded in France in 1849. Also created in Sag Harbor was the Academy of the Sacred Heart on Division Street in the former mansion of Phineas Parker King which was demolished; its site now a public school.

The religious community is centered in the Cormaria Retreat House on Bay Street, the former home of Frank Havens.

SAINT JAMES EPISCOPAL CHAPEL

On Noyac Road, adjacent to the Elizabeth A. Morton National Wildlife Refuge, built in 1912 and awarded landmark status in 2002.

SLEIGHT'S HILL

In Sag Harbor at the top of High Street and named for one of the town's most distinguished families. A stone monument at the crest states: *Upon This Spot Stood An American Fort 1812.* Another stone monument at the intersection with Rysam Street marks the Rysam-Sleight vault. The Sleights were shipowners and involved in the whaling business, leaders in various endeavors. Brindley Dering Sleight was the editor of the *Sag Harbor Corrector*, the newspaper that preceded *The Sag Harbor Express*.

STANTON HOUSE

A Greek Revival house next to the Civil War Monument in Sag Harbor, built in 1840 by the father of Oscar Stanton who was a young Naval officer with Perry on the *Susquehanna* in 1853 in Japan. He served with the Union Navy in the Civil War, became an admiral and died in 1924. A destroyer, DE-247 was named for him and saw action in World War II. His mother was Elizabeth Havens Cooper.

The Stanton House was built on the site of a small cottage where Captain David Hand (who had five wives) lived. The cottage was moved to Church Street.

TERRY DRIVE

Thomas Terry was a member of the Howell Company that came to North Sea in 1640 and founded Southampton. Earlier members of this distinguished family had arrived at Plymouth Rock. Terry Drive, in Sag Harbor, is east of Havens Beach. Fort Terry is on Plum Island.

TOLL GATE

In 1842, the Bridgehampton Sag Harbor Turnpike, under state charter, became a toll road, called The Sag Harbor and Bull's Head Turnpike. In 1906 it was taken over by the town and the toll gate was removed.

TREDWELL LANE

In Noyac. Built in 1989 by Timothy Covert Tredwell.

TROUT POND

Obadiah Rogers probably dammed a stream called the Noyack River around 1686 and built a mill on the spillway. William Pelletreau tells us that these ponds were bought by G.W. Thompson of Oakland, California in 1874 and he "improved them at great expense as trout ponds and made the area 'one of the most beautiful places on Long Island.'" Once called Mill Pond. There's a Trout Pond Road in Noyac.

UMBRELLA HOUSE

In Sag Harbor, on Division Street, so named because of its distinctive overhanging roof. It's said to be the oldest building in the village (18th century). During the Revolution it served as a barracks for British soldiers and was struck by a cannonball in the War of 1812 when the British attempted to land troops and burn the town.

UNION STREET

The street in Sag Harbor that effects a union with the Bridgehampton Turnpike (Main Street at that point) and Division Street, the main road to East Hampton.

The John Jermain Library was built on the corner of Main Street and Union Street in 1910, a gift to the village of Sag Harbor by Mrs. Russell Sage, widow of Russell Sage, whose summer home across Main Street is now the Whaling Museum.

President Chester A. Arthur spent some time in the summer of 1882 as a guest in the large Victorian house on the south side of the street, then owned by Stephen French who was the Police Commissioner of New York. This house, built in 1796, was once owned by Lester Beebe, a whaling captain, and later by Dr. Morley Lewis.

WEGWAGONUCK

According to Tooker, that part of Sag Harbor, east of Division Street which was the site of an Indian settlement marked by heaps of shells. The word meaning "place at the foot of the hill."

WHALEBONE LANDING

Indicated on maps as early as 1712 in Noyac west of Jessup's Neck on Peconic Bay, suggesting that in early times whales ventured into the bay. The bay's shallow water and sandy bottom were selected as the testing site in 1899 for John P. Holland's experimental submarines, based in New Suffolk on the North Fork.

Whalers' Church, Sag Harbor

WHALERS' CHURCH

On Union Street in Sag Harbor, the town's First Presbyterian Church was designed by Minard Lafever and built in 1843. This historic edifice had a 135-foot steeple which was blown off during the 1938 hurricane. It was named because the tall steeple was the first sight viewed by returning whaleships. A National Historic Landmark.

WICKATUCK DRIVE

In Noyac, opposite Long Beach Road. Derived from the Indian *Weeckatuck* meaning "end of the woods."

WICKATUCK SPRING

Very early records indicate that there was a spring at Noyac close to Long Beach at or below the bluff here (west of what was once a pavilion owned by McNally). W.W. Tooker in 1893 is said to have carved "Weekatuck, 1637-1893" on a nearby stone. The spring appears to have vanished. Across Noyac Road from the area is a Spring Road.

WIDOW GAVITTS ROAD

An extension of Toppings Path in Bridgehampton, a town trustee road which once ran south from Sagg Road past Crooked Pond to Haines Path. Now part of the Long Pond Greenbelt. The Gavitts owned a farm in the locality in 1813.

WILLIAM MULVIHILL PRESERVE

Land purchased by Southampton Town in 2006, with the assistance of The Nature Conservancy, following the author's death in 2004, for open space, habitat protection and groundwater preservation. Over twenty-five acres of woodland and wetlands, the sanctuary hosts rare wildflowers and salamanders and a myriad of amphibians, birds, mammals and plant life. Beloved to the author and his family, the creation of the preserve was a long-time dream of the author of this book.

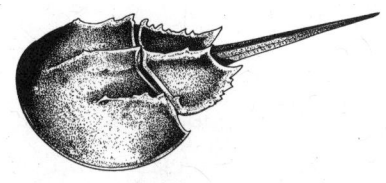

NORTH HAVEN

ACTORS COLONY ROAD

Leads off Ferry Road in North Haven. William Farnum (1876-1953), a famous actor in the early 1900s, had a home here, also Robert Edeson (1868-1931) and William Crane. Frank Case, owner of the Algonquin Hotel in Manhattan, a gathering place for actors and writers, also had a summer home here. By coincidence, Michael Caine, the British actor, stayed at a house there while acting in *Sweet Liberty* (1986), filmed in Sag Harbor.

BARCLAY'S

The Barclay estate on the west side of North Haven fronting on Noyac Bay, owned in the 19th century by B.J. Barclay.

CORWIN ROAD

The Corwin family was one of the early settlers off Ferry Road. Seth Corwin was a signer of the 1842 document which changed the name of Hog Neck to North Haven. Captain Lewis Jagger Corwin, a whaler, built the Old Schoolhouse on Payne Avenue.

EDESON LANE

A non-existent road which appears on some maps and is misspelled "Edison" Lane. It once ran from Actors Colony Road to Shelter Island Sound in North Haven. Named for Robert Edeson (1868-1931), a stage actor, and from 1914-1931, a movie actor in 63 films. Edeson called his estate Strongheart after a 1905 play in which he starred.

FAHYS ROAD

Joseph Fahys (1832-1925), born in France, created Fahys Watchworks (1881), later Bulova Watch Factory (1936), which for many years was Sag Harbor's major employer. He married Maria L'Hommedieu Payne. Fahys Road is in North Haven where Fahys once owned a thousand acres, including what is now called West Banks. He gave the Barclay estate to his daughter and son-in-law.

FERRY ROAD CEMETERY

On the west side of Ferry Road in North Haven. Many monuments are Connecticut Valley sandstone.

GLEASON POINT

In North Haven fronting on Shelter Island Sound facing Shelter Island, near Janet Creek. G. H. Gleason owned this site in the 1800s.

HAVENS CEMETERY

Owned by North Haven. At North Haven Point off Ferry Road.

HOGONECK LANE

Off North Haven Way. Hogoneck was the name for all of North Haven until 1842 when the inhabitants voted to change it to one they believed was more appealing. We can presume that the island was used as an isolated summer range for hogs, horses, sheep and cattle.

Near Janet Creek, by Gleason Point

JANET CREEK

Noted in error on some maps as Genet Creek. This North Haven estuary is named for Janet Havens (1769-1852), daughter of Constant and Abigail Havens and great-granddaughter of Jonathan Havens, one of the earliest settlers of North Haven. Janet was born in a nearby farmhouse and never married. Seventy acres of tidal marshland around the creek is owned by the town.

MAUNEKEA STREET

In North Haven off Ferry Road. The name should properly be Mauna Kea Street in that it was named for the Hawaiian volcano by Captain Lewis Jagger Corwin, a 19th century whaling ship captain who presumably visited Hawaii and saw the volcano. His Greek Revival house stands on the corner of Ferry Road and Maunekea Street.

MAYCROFT

A waterside summer house built in 1885 by James Herman Aldrige, a lawyer who lived in Manhattan. The architect was Edward Delano Lindsey. Aldrige was a key figure in creating Sag Harbor's Episcopal Church. A memorial window, *Jesus' Presentation in the Temple*, was created by the renowned Louis Comfort Tiffany. Aldrige also created the Maycroft Cup, still used by the Sag Harbor Yacht Club. In 1921 the 42-acre property was bequeathed to the Episcopal Diocese. Since 1994, the estate is on the State Register of Historic Places.

Mrs. Aldrige's first name was May. *Croft* in Old English means an enclosed field, especially with a cottage.

NORTH HAVEN

Now a village, this near-island was once called Hog Neck until 1842 when several families (Paynes, Hildreths, Edwards) agreed to change the name to one that would "sound better to modern ears." A bridge eventually linked North Haven with Sag Harbor. A more recent bridge spanned Polles Creek, an extension of the Cove. A ferry crosses to Shelter Island.

NORTH HAVEN POINT

A large area, now a housing development. One hundred acres was once owned by the Pallotine Fathers, a Catholic order.

POLLES CREEK

Once considered the boundary between North Haven (Hog Neck) and Noyac. An extension of the Sag Harbor Cove. A causeway built over it in 1902 by Charles Lamott permits the tidal flow of water. The bridge was demolished in 2002. The creek runs behind the beach almost to Sunset Beach Road. The origin of the name is unknown.

RYDER'S POND

Adjacent to Sunset Beach Road in North Haven and named for the Ryder family who lived in the vicinity.

STOCK FARM

In North Haven. An early owner was Jonathan Havens of Shelter Island. The farm was identified with the raising of cattle and horses.

TYNDAL POINT

That point of land in North Haven east of Ferry Road which reaches toward Shelter Island. George and William Tyndall were the original ferrymen who, before the age of the automobile, used a flat-bottomed scow with oars and sail to transport people and carts across the channel.

Tyndal Road could be considered an extension of Ferry Road where it joins Short Beach Road in North Haven.

BRIDGEHAMPTON AND SAGAPONACK

AUSTIN'S POND

A Southampton Town trustee's pond south of Scuttlehole Road in Bridgehampton. Once known as Goldfish Pond because it had been stocked with goldfish, *Carassius auratus*, a non-native fish which upset the ecological balance.

BEEBEE WINDMILL

At the two-acre John E. Berwind Memorial Village Green in Bridgehampton on Ocean Road and Hildreth Road. Built in Sag Harbor in 1820 for Lester Beebee by Samuel Schellenger, it was transported to other locations by various owners until it became a gift of the Berwind estate. Said to be the last surviving iron-geared windmill in America.

Captain Lester Beebee (1754-1832) served in the Revolution and is buried in Sag Harbor's Old Burying Ground.

BLANK LANE

It was the practice of the early Town Proprietors to set aside a "blank lot" to be sold by them to cover the cost of creating a new division of land. Blank Lot Lane, in 1712, was the original name for this byway now running from Deerfield Road to Head of the Pond Road.

BREEZE HILL

The highest place on Scuttlehole Road, in Bridgehampton close to Shorts Pond. It might have been called Wind Mill Hill after a mill built by John Wick who died in 1719.

BRIDGEHAMPTON

A bridge built by Ezekiel Sanford, across the northern edge of Sagg Pond, was part of the original road from Southampton to East Hampton. Nathan Sandford (1777-1838), a descendant of Ezekiel, became a U.S. Senator.

Bridgehampton was once called Feversham. The Bridgehampton

Sag Harbor Turnpike was, in 1690, called the Cart Path to Great Meadows, the first name for Sag Harbor.

BULLHEAD LANE

Off Hildreth Avenue in Bridgehampton. Probably named because it's in the vicinity of the Bullshead Inn which gave the name to the area around the road to Sag Harbor, once called Bullshead Turnpike.

BULLSHEAD TURNPIKE

Now known as the Bridgehampton Sag Harbor Turnpike, this highway was built by the Sag Harbor and the Bulls Head Turnpike Company in 1837 and was a toll road owned by stockholders. The rates were five cents one way for a wagon drawn by two horses, two cents for each additional horse, mule or ox. For every coach or phaeton, the charge was twenty cents. A horse led or ridden was one cent. Bulls Head gave its name to the large inn built on the eastern edge of Bridgehampton's Main Street. A similar toll road ran from Sag Harbor to East Hampton.

Ernest Clowes tells us the name originated when someone hung on a tree a sign on which a bull's head was painted.

BUTTER LANE

In Bridgehampton between Mitchell Lane and Lumber Lane. The name might be derived from Pierce Butler who owned a farm in the locality.

COOKS LANE

In Bridgehampton north off Scuttlehole Road. Major Silas Cook owned a house before 1750 just west of Shorts Pond (Scuttlehole Pond).

CORWITH HOMESTEAD

On Main Street in Bridgehampton, now the headquarters of the Bridgehampton Historical Society and a museum. Behind the house are barns containing antique engines and farm implements and a wheelwright shop. David Corwith arrived on the South Fork in 1665, the first of a widespread and distinguished family. The name—with origins in Cornwall—was originally Carwitham.

Corwith Avenue links the Montauk Highway with Railroad Avenue.

FAIRFIELD POND

The pond in Sagaponack west of Fairfield Pond Road, close to the ocean beach. In 1726, Pelletreau notes a transaction from Josiah Topping to Theophilus Pierson for land "at a place commonly called Fairfield, bounded east by a pond."

GIBSON LANE

Runs south from Sagaponack Main Street to the ocean. Once called Old Beach Road. Named for Hanson Cox

Gibson (1835-1922), a lawyer from New York, who owned 48 ocean-front acres here in 1889.

HAMPTON HOUSE

At the junction of Ocean Road and Main Street in Bridgehampton, built around 1820 by Abraham Topping Rose (1792-1857). It was bought in 1838 by Nathaniel Rogers (1787-1844), a miniaturist painter of renown whose work is in the Metropolitan Museum. The large Greek Revival house with Ionic columns became The Hampton House in 1855 and catered to summer visitors. Now owned by the Town of Southampton.

HAYGROUND

An area in Bridgehampton bordering Mecox Bay. The marshy land was a source of "salt hay", *Spartina alterniflora* or *Spartina patens*, which, in the winter, provided grazing for cattle and other livestock. Hayground Cove empties into Mecox Bay at Water Mill.

HAYNE'S POND

Named after the Haynes family, just north of Scuttlehole Road in Bridgehampton. Also called Scuttlehole Pond.

HEDGES LANE

In Sagaponack, created in 1926, linking Sagaponack Main Street with Town Line Road. Deacon David Hedges built a house in the area in 1775. Named for Benjamin Hedges who died in 1890.

HULL LANE

A short road linking Main Street with Ocean Road in Bridgehampton and named for John Hull who, in 1865, owned The Atlantic House, a hotel where Saint Ann's Episcopal Church is located.

HUNTINGTON CROSSWAY

Connects the Bridgehampton Sag Harbor Turnpike with the eastern segment of Scuttlehole Road which in former times was called Huntington Pass. Harry Sleight wrote that "The north end of Lumber Lane, at Bridgehampton, was called the settlement of Huntington."

JEHU'S POND

South of Hayne's Pond close to Scuttlehole Road in Bridgehampton. Named after Jehu Rugg, a black man who once lived in the vicinity.

KELLIS POND

The name probably came from Kelly's Pond (1651) or Cally's Pond mentioned in a 1700 deed transferring a parcel of land "at Mecox, joining to a pond commonly called Cally's Pond" (Pelletreau). This pond once drained into Calf Creek.

MECOX

A Bridgehampton—Hayground district as well as 1200-acre Mecox Bay. Tooker believes that the origin of the word is Indian, derived from the name of an Indian *Secommecock* who signed the Southampton Indian deed in 1640.

MERCHANTS PATH

Henry P. Hedges tells us that "Merchant Howell cut a road (1712) through the woods from Poxabogue to Northwest whereby to cart his goods." Northwest Creek was the first harbor for East Hampton but was displaced by the port of Sag Harbor which could handle ships with deeper drafts. Part of this road has become a section of Swamp Road off the East Hampton Sag Harbor Turnpike.

MILITIA GREEN

In Bridgehampton on the west side of Ocean Road near Montauk Highway. Also called Triangular Commons. A place where Bridgehampton men trained for service. A monument reads:

Triangular Commons Training Grounds
of Militia of Eastern Long Island in Colonial Days
1649-1776
Bridge-hampton, New York.

MINDEN

An estate on the east side of Ocean Road in Bridgehampton, the summer home of John E. Berwind. Minden is a historic town in Germany on the Weser River.

MITCHELL LANE

Links Scuttlehole Road with Halsey Lane in Bridgehampton. John Mitchell owned acerage here in 1716.

MONTROSE LANE

A street in Hayground named for Monterossa, a town in Italy where the ancestors of developer Lawrence (Lawrence Court) Ingolia came from.

NAROD BLVD.

In Hayground off Mecox Road close to Calf Creek. The builder of many houses here was named Doran, which backwards, spells Narod.

NARROW LANE

The name was changed from Cook's Lane, running east from Lumber Lane under the railroad tracks in Poxabogue to Sagg Road. Cook is an ancient name on the South Fork. In 1750 Abraham Cook owned land west of Poxabogue Pond.

NEW LIGHT LANE

In the early 1700s, a religious upheaval called the Great Awakening resulted in a rift in the Christian churches of Colonial America. Spurred by evangelists such as Johnathan Edwards and George Whitefield, the religious communities polarized as the more cosmopolitan rationalists found themselves challenged by the raw emotionalism of the awakened reformists. The latter became known as the New Lights and established many New Light churches in New England and Long Island.

New Light Lane in Hayground was named because of a local meetinghouse identified with this religious schism.

NEWMAN AVENUE

In Bridgehampton and named for Rev. Arthur Newman of the local Presbyterian church, the pastor from 1883 to his death in 1924.

NORRIS LANE

In Bridgehampton's Poxabogue area running from the Montauk Highway to Narrow Lane. A 17th century name left by Robert and Nathan Norris.

OCEAN ROAD

In Bridgehampton running south from the Montauk Highway to the ocean and called in 1670 the Path Into the Woods. Later named Ye Cart Path to Beach, then Beach Road and in 1850 called Ocean Road, according to William Donald Halsey.

PARSONAGE LANE

In Sagaponack, running east from Sagaponack Main Street to Town Line Road. Parsonage lands were, in early times, those areas set aside by the Proprietors, for use by the minister.

Abigail Fithian Halsey tells us that 20 acres near First Neck Lane were so designated in early Southampton. Southampton's first minister Reverend Abraham Pierson graduated in 1632 from Cambridge University and served from 1640 to 1647. His son became the first president of Yale.

PAUL'S LANE

Built around 1680 and named after Paul Halsey, this road links Mecox Road with New Light Lane in Bridgehampton.

POTASH POND

On the Bridgehampton Golf Course and taking the name from the site where potassium carbonate was created by evaporating the lixivium of wood ashes from iron pots. Large amounts of water were needed which placed the establishment near the pond. Potash was used to make soap.

POXABOGUE

A pond close to the Montauk Highway and a district of Bridgehampton. Now part of the county's Poxabogue Pond Preserve (26 acres). According to Tooker, the name is derived from *Paugasa-baug* meaning a pond that widens. This is true of Poxabog Pond which expands its surface during periods of heavy rainfall and contracts during droughts. When high, the pond water overflows and runs under the highway to Sagg Swamp—a Nature Conservancy area—and to Sagg Pond.

The first house was built in 1712 by Edward Howell and his wife, Abigail Sanford, whose father Ezekial Sanford had built the bridge across Sagg Pond and so gave Bridgehampton its name.

POXABOGUE – EVERGREEN CEMETERY

On Montauk Highway and Sagg Main Street. The first burial was that of Martha Pierson in 1773.

QUIMBY LANE

In Bridgehampton, off Ocean Road, named for one of the original summer visitors, Edward Everett Quimby, who arrived in 1877 and bought land on Sagaponack Pond.

SAGAPONACK

An area east of Bridgehampton known as Sagg until 1889 as well as Sagg Pond and Sagg Swamp. Josiah Stanborough built the first house here in 1656. W.W. Tooker credits the origin of the name to *Sagga*, an edible tuber eaten by the Indians.

The first land allotment here in 1653 was to Josiah Stanborough.

SAGG SWAMP PRESERVE

A 90-acre holding of The Nature Conservancy north of Sagg Road in Bridgehampton, created in 1967 by the generosity of Carrol Wainright, Edward Mathews, John Maynard, Augusta Poe Maynard and Walter Maynard.

Fresh water from the swamp runs south into Sagaponack Pond.

SAM'S CREEK

A finger of Mecox Bay, east of the Job's Lane bridge. Ernest Clowes says that the creek was named after an Indian "who frequented the hospitable firesides of the early Mecox settlers who, for reasons unknown, once jumped into that body of water." Architect Norman Jaffe designed six houses along the creek. Also, Sam's Creek Road off Ocean Road.

SAWASETT AVENUE

Off the Bridgehampton Sag Harbor Turnpike. W.W. Tooker cites many similar spellings of this Indian name meaning "at the place of small pines". The Indian word for Port Jefferson was *Sowasett*.

SAYRE PARK

A seven-acre town owned parcel in Bridgehampton fronting on Snake Hollow Road and running to Long Pond, north of the railroad tracks.

Given to the Town of Southampton in 1992 by Thomas E. Sayre, a descendant of Thomas Sayre, born in England in 1597.

SCUTTLEHOLE ROAD

A scuttlehole was another name for a trap door in the roof of a house that was handy in case of a chimney fire or to simply view the sea. Scuttlehole Road runs through flat potato land, and affords a view of the Bridgehampton ocean that is two or three miles away.

At one time, this meandering road was called Head of the Pond Road. Scuttle Hole was once a district within Bridgehampton. An old name in 1679 was Huntington Path.

SHORTS POND

A kettle pond just north of Scuttlehole Road in Bridgehampton, once called Scuttlehole Pond. Also Haynes Pond.

SLADE POND

Close to the west side of the turnpike in Bridgehampton, north of the railroad tracks; about two acres, shown and named on a 1700 map. *Slade* is an ancient English word, now obsolete, and, according to the Oxford English Dictionary, refers to a greensward or boggy land. Mistakenly called Slate Pond.

STRAIGHT BEACH

In Bridgehampton at the south end of Ocean Road.

STRONG'S LANE

Links Hayground Road and Scuttlehole Road in Bridgehampton. Charles Strong was a Town resident in 1661.

TOPPINGS FIELD COURT

Off Hildreth Lane in Bridgehampton. The Topping name is one of the oldest and most distinguished on the South Fork.

TOPPINGS PATH

Off Sagg Road, close to Crooked Pond, north of Bridgehampton. The Toppings are an old and distinguished family on the South

Fork. One of the early whaling captains commemorated on The Broken Mast Monument in Sag Harbor's Oakland Cemetery was Richard Topping, of Bridgehampton, master of the *Thorn* who died at sea in 1836 when he was 29. Two Toppings served in the Civil War, M. Howell as a Captain in the 100th New York Infantry and William Owen, a Lieutenant in the 7th Wisconsin who was killed at Fredericksburg. Thomas Topping, in 1662, purchased from the Indians a very large parcel of land "west of Shinecock."

TREES LANE

A road in Sagaponack close to the ocean in what was the Topping farm, thought to be the oldest (around 1656) continuously owned and operating farm in the state until the 1970s. Now filled with houses. The developer was James Trees.

WICK'S TAVERN

A metal sign on the corner of the Montauk Highway and the Bridgehampton Sag Harbor Turnpike reads:

> *Wick's Tavern*
> *Built in 1686 by John Wick*
> *and used by American and*
> *English soldiers during the*
> *American Revolution*

NORTHWEST

BARCELONA NECK

Tooker was unable to trace the name to Indian origins. He mentions a sea captain who claimed that the name was taken from the Spanish city of Barcelona because the high bluffs there resemble those of this point of wooded land east of Sag Harbor. Previously known as Russell's Neck, named for the original family that settled here in the 1700s.

In 1989, the 341-acre peninsula—the site of the Sag Harbor Golf Club—was acquired by New York State.

BUFFALO WALLOW

In Northwest and north of Northwest Road. So named because David Gardiner (according to Jeannette Edwards Rattray) once "kept buffalo" here and on his farm in East Hampton. The origin of these animals—we assume that they were western bison—is unstated.

CHATFIELD'S HOLE

On the east side of Two Holes of Water Road in Northwest. A hole is an old name for a pond.

In 1976 the town of East Hampton placed a monument here as a bicentennial marker which reads:

> *Chatfield's Hole*
> *Named after one of the early settlers*
> *Thomas Chatfield*
> *who was Collector of the Port 1668 and Town Clerk*
> *in the early 1700s*

CUFFEE'S BEACH

On Northwest Creek across from Barcelona Point. Also known as Stratton's Beach. Wickham Cuffee (1826-1915) was a Shinnecock Indian. Reverend Paul Cuffee (1757-1812) was a Christian preacher at the Shinnecock Reservation. Stratton is an original settler name.

EDWARDS' HOLE ROAD

William Edwards arrived in East Hampton in 1650 or 1651. His wife came from Maidstone, in England. An ancient, widespread and distinguished family name. Edwards' Hole (a pond or vernal pond) Road in Northwest links Swamp Road with the East Hampton Sag Harbor Turnpike.

Caldwell Edwards (1841-1922), born in Sag Harbor, died there and is buried in Oakland Cemetery. He moved to Montana in 1864, was elected to Congress in 1901.

ELLYBROOK

An estuary in Northwest once called Alewife Brook that flows into Northwest Harbor from Alewife Brook Pond. An alewife is a member of the herring family. An old name for Cedar Point was Alewife Brook Neck.

Also, Ellybrook Road which ends close to the mouth of the estuary. This area is now Cedar Point County Park.

GRACE ESTATE PRESERVE

At Northwest Harbor. Now an East Hampton Town park, named for W.R. Grace (1878-1943), a corporate official who bought the land in 1910. In 1985, a Town referendum allowed most of the 516 acres—threatened by proposed development—to be preserved. Off Old Northwest Road, including Scoy Pond.

Captain David Hand's grave alongside his five wives in Oakland Cemetery, Sag Harbor

HAND'S CREEK

A small body of water, flowing into Three Mile Harbor, believed to be named after John Hand around 1670. Also Hand Lane in Amagansett and Stephen Hands Path in Wainscott.

Robert Cushman Murphy identifies Hand as a *Mayflower* name dating back to an ancestor who came to Plymouth Rock. Other very old South Fork names include: Bayles, Conklin, Davis, Dayton, Hallock, Havens, Hawkins, Hedges, Helme, Homan, Hopkins, Hulse, Jayne, Jones, Ketcham, Miller, Phillips, Platt, Randall, Roe, Satterly, Scudder, Smith, Strong, Terry, Tooker, Warner and Wicks.

Josiah Hand lived "at the Brickilns" and fought with George

Washington at the Battle of Long Island and at Trenton. Natty Bumpo, a fictional character created by novelist James Fenimore Cooper who spent time in Sag Harbor, is supposedly modeled on David Hand, a sea captain who died in 1840 and outlived all of his five wives.

HEDGES BANKS

The high banks or sandy cliffs in Northwest took their name from Ebenezer Hedges or William Hedges who settled East Hampton in 1652. Captain Hiram B. Hedges commanded the whaling ship *Josephine* which in 1846-1849 circled the globe.

Hedges Banks Drive skirts Gardiner's Bay, running off North Hollow Road to the county park at Cedar Point.

JASON'S ROCK

A large glacial erratic off Bull Path in Northwest. Jason Hoopte was an Indian in the 19th century who walked each day from East Hampton to Sag Harbor and would stop here to drink from rainwater that collected in a depression at the top of the megalith.

KIRK'S PLACE

Josiah Kirk, from Ireland, bought a bay-front farm in Northwest in the 1800s. The street is now encompassed within the Grace Estate Preserve, off Alewife Brook Road.

LAFARGE'S LANDING

At the end of Old House Landing Road in Northwest, north of Sammis Beach. A house owned by Henry LaFarge appears on an 1873 map of Northwest. The name might have evolved from LaSage, an early Huguenot name that became Sage.

LONE GRAVE ROAD

Benjamin Hubbard was buried here in 1789. He was only 22 and perished from smallpox. The road is on an East Hampton Town Trustee Road which ends at the intersection of Swamp Road and Bull Path in Northwest.

NORTHWEST

Once known as Alewife Brook Neck and, in colonial times, one of the more remote, unsettled and heavily forested regions in the northwestern area of East Hampton Town, bounded by Northwest Harbor, Northwest Creek, Gardiner's Bay and Three Mile Harbor. Once a hamlet (with a schoolhouse) which vanished with the rise of the port at Sag Harbor. Large areas, such as Barcelona, are county parkland. Northwest Harbor is a habitat for the diamondback terrapin (*Macalemys terra*).

PENNYPACKER AVENUE

Off Old Northwest Road in Northwest and named for Town Historian Morton Pennypacker whose collection of Long

Island history is housed in the East Hampton Library. Pennypacker wrote *General Washington's Spies on Long Island and in New York* (1939).

The East Hampton Town Board, under pressure from residents, changed the historic name to Country Lane.

PHOEBE SCOY HIGHWAY

A road in Northwest that runs off North West Landing Road. An original 18th century settler family in this area was named Van Scoy and once called Van Scoyack, then Scoy.

POWDER HILL

Said to have been a hiding place for gunpowder during the War of 1812 when British warships were in Gardiner's Bay blockading South Fork ports. In Northwest. Also called Mile Hill.

RATTLESNAKE CREEK

A small stream or drain which originates east of the Sag Harbor East Hampton Turnpike to empty into Little Northwest Creek. A reminder that timber rattlesnakes, *Crotalus horridus*, existed on Long Island but, like the wolves and bobcats (*Lynx rufus*), were exterminated by the early settlers. Once called Tanbark Creek.

SAINT REGIS COURT

Camp St. Regis was a summer boys' camp in Northwest, created in 1937 by the Kennedy family on property known as Monk's Farm. Destroyed by fire, the camp rose Phoenix-like at a new site on Three Mile Harbor and is now called Boys and Girls Harbor. The road name, off Mile High Road in Northwest, remains.

SAMMIS BEACH

Sometimes, by mistake, called "Sammy's Beach," the error compounded by mapmakers. The beach, fronting on Gardiner's Bay, is part of the sandy arm that embraces Three Mile Harbor. Sammis is an old family name on Long Island.

SCOY'S POND

A pond in Northwest (Alewife Brook Neck), near Ellybrook Road; the name comes from an original settler family named Van Schaik (later Van Scoy) who were numerous in this area in the 18th century. The family came from Holland and once spelled the name Van Scoyack. Isaac Van Scoy, the first of his name, settled in the primal forest in 1757 and married Mercy Edwards, who bore 15 children. During the Revolutionary War, Isaac killed a British sailor who was looting his home, was taken as a prisoner to an English warship at Sag Harbor and, while awaiting trial, escaped with the help of friends.

SPRINGY BANKS

In 1731-32, from *Memoranda* of the Journal of the Trustees: "Indians commonly dwell at Springy Banks, Three Mile Harbor, in summer time." Springy Banks Road runs north from Three Mile Harbor Road in East Hampton. Named for the abundance of springs in the area.

TWO HOLES OF WATER ROAD

Links Swamp Road in Northwest with Stephen Hands Path, named for two kettle holes or ponds in the area.

VAN SCOY CEMETERY

In Northwest off the south side of Swamp Road, near Bull Path, surrounded by a white fence just visible from the road and close to a stone plaque noting the original school. A private burial ground for members of the early Van Scoy family.

WHEELOCK WALK

In Northwest, linking Stephen Hands Path with Hand's Creek Road. Named for John Hall Wheelock (1885-1978). An editor at Scribner's, he also wrote poetry and literary criticism. Recipient of many awards including the Bollingen Prize and honored by the Academy of American Poets. *Verse by Two Undergraduates* 1905 (with Van Wyck Brooks). *Love and Liberation* 1913. *The Bright Doom* 1927.

EAST HAMPTON

AMY'S LANE

Amy Miller Mulford (born 1732) was the wife of Ezekial Mulford (1727-1819), a Revolutionary War captain who served with Colonel Josiah Smith's regiment of eastern Suffolk militiamen. Ezekial was Amy's second husband and they had seven children.

Amy's Lane connects Pantigo Road with Hither Lane.

APAQUOQUE

A district in East Hampton village south of Lily Pond Lane.

The Indian word, according to W.W. Tooker, refers to a type of cattail rush or wetland reed (*Typha latifolia*) which Indians used to make mats and baskets. Also Apaquogue Road which runs off Georgica Road.

BAITING HOLLOW ROAD

In East Hampton Village, off Georgica Road. *Baiting* is an old English word associated with feeding or eating. This area was, perhaps, a place where livestock were enclosed to graze.

BEECHER-HAND HOUSE

Since 1994 the Village Hall of East Hampton at 86 Main Street. Built in the middle of the 18th century. Bought, in 1800, by Reverend Lyman Beecher. In 1810 it was sold to Abraham Hand.

BUCKSKILL ROAD

Poggatacut, a chief of the Manhassets died in 1651. His body was brought from Shelter Island to Montauk and the party transporting the body rested somewhere on the way to East Hampton. Buckskill is derived from the Indian word *buc-usk-kill* meaning the resting place. Buckskill Road runs south from Route 114 crossing Stephen Hands Path.

BUELL LANE

In East Hampton Village running from Cove Hollow Road

to Main Street. Reverend Samuel Buell (1716-1798) who graduated from Yale in 1741, was an early East Hampton minister, an outspoken leader during the British occupation. His successor was Lyman Beecher. Samuel and Jerusha's daughter Jerusha Buell married David Gardiner of Gardiner's Island.

BURNT POINT

A neck of land on Georgica Pond named because at the turn of the century a fire devastated the forest here.

CALF PASTURE LANE

Grazing land in East Hampton set aside for the personal use of the village's minister. Now called Ocean Avenue.

CLINTON ACADEMY

In East Hampton, built in 1784, the first college preparatory school in the state was named for Governor Clinton of New York. The first headmaster was Reverend Samuel Buell. Now a museum. Anna Symmes (1775-1864) from the North Fork, a student here, became the wife of President William Henry Harrison (1773-1841) and grandmother of Benjamin Harrison (1833-1901), the 23rd president. Donated in 1921 by Mrs. Lorenzo Woodhouse to the East Hampton Historical Society.

There's a Clinton Academy Lane in Amagansett.

COOPER LANE

Off Newtown Lane in East Hampton Village and named for Thomas Cooper who built a house there in 1651.

THE CREEKS

A 60-acre estate on Georgica Pond once owned by Adele and Albert Herter whose son Christian A. Herter (1895-1966) was Secretary of State during part of the Eisenhower presidency. The house was later owned by Alfonso Ossario, the artist. Noted for its extensive and exotic gardens and named for the small creeks that are part of the pond.

CROSS HIGHWAY

In East Hampton Town there are at least a half dozen roads bearing this name and were so named because they link one road with another.

DAVID'S LANE

In East Hampton Village off Main Street, running to Egypt Lane. Named for David Huntting (1851-1891).

DIVINITY HILL

An area around Cottage Avenue in East Hampton named because it became identified with the residences of clergymen such as the Reverend T. DeWitt Talmadge.

DREW LANE

Off Lily Pond Lane in East Hampton. John Drew (1853-1927) was once called the Beau Brummel of the American stage. He had a home on Lily Pond Lane. His niece was Ethel Barrymore.

EAST HAMPTON

The village might well be "America's Most Beautiful Village" as it has been described. East Hampton Town includes all the villages east of Sagaponack—Town Line Road—to Montauk. Division Street in Sag Harbor separates Southampton Town and East Hampton Town. The first "Hampton" was Southampton (1640) followed by the next township to the east, hence the name. Hampton is an ancient name brought from England.

The earliest settler was Lion Gardiner.

EAST HAMPTON NATURE TRAIL AND BIRD SANCTUARY

A 25-acre wild area in the village on both sides of Hook Dreen, bisected by Huntting Lane. Created by an initial gift from Mary Leland Kennedy Woodhouse (1951) and enlarged by gifts of land from Miss Mary Rogers (1978) and Mrs. Roland V. Christie (1992).

The preserve includes eight swampy acres along Egypt Lane

and Fithian Lane donated to the village in 1934 by Matilda Donoho. The dreen carries water into Hook Pond.

EAST HAMPTON VILLAGE NORTH BURYING GROUND

At the north end of Main Street one will find epitaphs for ancient families such as Wickham, Baker, Hutchinson, Parsons and others.

Grave of Lion Gardiner, South Burying Ground, East Hampton

Site of First Church, East Hampton

EAST HAMPTON VILLAGE SOUTH BURYING GROUND

One of the oldest and historically significant cemeteries in the nation at Main Street, close to Town Pond. Here one read epitaphs of the earliest families on the South Fork: Conkling, Gardiner, Buell, Huntting, Mulford, Stratton, Osborne, Miller, Fithian, King, Tallmadge, Dayton, Davis, Hedges, Chatfield, Barnes and others.

The most imposing monument is that of Lion Gardiner (1663-1799), an ornate creation of James Renwick who designed St. Patrick's Cathedral in Manhattan.

Other Gardiners buried here include New York State Senator David Gardiner, whose daughter Julia married sitting President John Tyler. David's grandson, once a Confederate soldier, is buried here as well.

EGYPT LANE

Everett T. Rattray suggests that this East Hampton Village byway is so named because "Down Egypt" was biblically dark and swampy and that in colonial times the low-lying area justified its name.

Frederick Childe Hassam (1859-1935), a painter and etcher of the Impressionist school, owned a house at 48 Egypt Lane which was built by William Barnes around 1722.

Also, Egypt Close off the Lane. Egypt Beach is the beach just east of the Maidstone Club.

FITHIAN LANE

A short street in East Hampton Village that links Main Street with Egypt Lane.

William Fithian was an early settler—if not the first—of East Hampton and is listed as living on the west side of Main Street. Fithian, according to Howell, was a Welshman, a soldier in Cromwell's Army who was present at the execution of

Charles I (1649). Proclaimed a regicide, he fled to America. Abigail Fithian Halsey wrote *In Old Southampton* in 1940.

FIVE ROD ROAD

Off Wainscott Main Street. A rod is an old term of lineal measurement equal to five and a half yards, possibly the width of the original road.

FREETOWN

An area of East Hampton village north of the railroad tracks segmented by Three Mile Harbor Road, Springs Fireplace Road and Hands Creek Road. This settlement, like Sag Harbor's Eastville, was once an enclave of freed slaves and Indians. Black slaves in New York State were given their freedom by a 1799 law passed by the State Legislature stipulating that slaves born after July 4, 1799 would be free when men became 27 and when women became 25.

FURTHER LANE

Perhaps it was originally called Farther Lane—more distant from the village of East Hampton than Middle Lane or Hither Lane. The west-to-east road closest to the ocean.

GARDINER-BROWN HOUSE

It was called the brown house because of its original color,

Gardiner Windmill, 1804, East Hampton

afterwards the Gardiner-Brown House. Built in 1740 by David Gardiner (1691-1751) and his wife Rachael Schellenger whose father Abraham owned the property.

The house was headquarters for the occupying English army during the Revolution, when Abraham Gardiner (a Tory) played host to Sir Henry Clinton, Admiral Arbuthnot (whose fleet was in Gardiner's Bay), Major Andre and others.

Located at 95 Main St., the Ladies' Village Improvement Society of East Hampton makes its headquarters here now, and has also held its annual Fair, established in 1896, on the Gardiner-Brown House lawn since 1990.

GAY LANE

An East Hampton byway that connects Main Street with Egypt Lane and is named after James E. Gay, a 19th century blacksmith whose place of business was located here.

Gay, with Patrick Lynch and 300 other Irish immigrants, survived the wreck of the *Catherine* in 1851 at Amagansett. The ship from Dublin was heading to New York.

GEORGICA

According to W.W. Tooker, *Jeorgkee* was an Indian who "went to sea to kill whales for Jacob Schillinger of East Hampton" and lived in the area near Georgica Pond. It is possible that the name could be a corruption of the English name of Georgia.

Originally a 290-acre pond, it was opened to the ocean to create a brackish environment. Such an opening, called a seapoose (many spellings), means little river. It's a publicly owned pond but, in recent years, public access has been blocked by private owners. Also, Georgica Neck, Georgica Creek, Georgica Close Road.

GOOSE POND

The early name for the East Hampton Village pond across from the old cemetery. The subject of an 1881 etching by Mary Nimmo Moran, the wife of the artist Thomas Moran.

GUILD HALL

On East Hampton's Main Street and designed by Aymar Embury II in 1931. Includes the John Drew Theater and several art galleries, given to the village by Mary Woodhouse, a member of the Maidstone Club and a patron of the arts.

HARDSCRABBLE

The general area between Sag Harbor and East Hampton around Stephen Hands Path. Hardscrabble Close is a dead end road that leads off the Turnpike. The origin of the name is imprecise but the historian John Fisk, in *The Beginnings of New England*, wrote that the "terse epithet" described an area inhabited by poor people.

HERRICK PARK

On Newtown Lane in East Hampton, given to the village in 1917 by James B. Ford to remember his sister Harriet F. Herrick, wife of Doctor Everett Herrick, a founder of the Maidstone Club. Mrs. Herrick was a very generous donor of books and money which created the local library.

HIGHWAY BEHIND THE LOTS

In the 1600s, the Proprietors of East Hampton laid out the home lots which were long narrow parcels. At some point a road was created behind these lots which had become sites for newer houses.

HOME SWEET HOME

Named from the song of the same name by John Howard Payne (1791-1852), this house built in 1660 on East Hampton's James Lane is now a museum filled with 18th century antiques. Payne was an actor and playwright and, from 1842 to 1845, the U.S. Consul in Tunis.

HOOK POND

In East Hampton, partially bordered by the Maidstone Club.

Like many ponds on the southern edge of the South Fork, it was created by barriers of sand carried by the ocean which trapped fresh water streams running to the sea. Hook Pond Lane. The name may have originated because of its shape.

HOOK WINDMILL

The first building bought by the Village of East Hampton in 1922. Built by Nathaniel Dominy IV in 1806—and still in working order—it was closed in 1908. Hook might be from the Dutch word *hoek* meaning corner.

HUNTTING LANE

Off Main Street in East Hampton and named for David H. Huntting who died in 1893. Rev. Nathaniel Huntting (Harvard, 1693) arrived in 1699 as the village's second minister. His home, now the Huntting Inn, was where nine generations of his descendants were born. During the Revolution it was an inn or public house.

JAMES LANE

In East Hampton, named for Rev. Thomas James Jr., first minister in East Hampton who died in 1696. James Springs in Springs once belonged to him.

JEFFREY'S LANE

In East Hampton, running south from James Lane. Charles

Jeffrey, an early summer resident, built a house here in 1872 with a view of Hook Pond.

JERICHO ROAD

South of the Montauk Highway near Georgica. Jericho was a hamlet laid out before 1700, originally part of the town of East Hampton. Early settlers were partial to Biblical names in giving place names and given names. Jericho was the ancient Canaanite city whose walls were miraculously destroyed when trumpets were blown.

LEARNED HAND'S COURT

Off Stephen Hands Path (west of the East Hampton Sag Harbor Turnpike) in East Hampton Town. Learned Hand (1872-1961) was a judge, U.S. Circuit Court, 2nd Circuit, 1924-51.

He was related to the ancient and distinguished Hand family of the South Fork. John Hand (died 1660) was one of the founders of East Hampton.

LILY POND LANE

In Apaquoque, in East Hampton Village, close to the ocean. In 1651 the small pond was called "The Littell Pond" perhaps because of its size.

LYMAN BEECHER HOUSE

In East Hampton Village on Main Street, named after Lyman Beecher (1775-1865), the fourth minister who graduated from Yale in 1797. His son was Henry Ward Beecher (1813-1887), the redoubtable orator and Protestant preacher. His daughter, Harriet Beecher Stowe (1811-1896), wrote *Uncle Tom's Cabin*.

MAIDSTONE

The original name for East Hampton which took its name from either Maidstone, a town in Kent and the origin of some of the early South Fork families or from John Maidstone of Boxted, England, a friend of John Winthrop. The East Hampton library was designed to resemble the library in Maidstone.

MAIDSTONE CLUB

When the original clubhouse burned to the ground, the directors, in 1924, built a new one on the ocean dunes. There was a golf course, a salt water swimming pool, beach cabanas. The artist Thomas Moran was a founder and at one time the club was the nexus of East Hampton summer society.

Maidstone is an area in England from which many original settlers or their ancestors came.

MCGUIRK STREET

Off Newtown Lane in East Hampton Village. In 1928 the land was transferred by Ellen McGuirk.

MILL HILL LANE

In East Hampton Village off Main Street. In 1677, a mill, said to be ox-powered, was erected for flouring purposes at the commencement of South Beach Lane.

MUCHMORE LANE

In East Hampton Village off Newtown Lane, named after Ernest B. Muchmore, a local businessman who died in 1929.

Mulford Homestead, East Hampton

MULFORD FARM

Built around 1650 and bought by Samuel Mulford in 1698, this property at 10 James Lane is maintained by the East Hampton Historical Society and preserves the ambiance of an original 17th century house in Maidstone, England, a restored 18th century barn and an herb garden.

NEWTOWN LANE

Because East Hampton's Main Street was originally called Town Street, its extension, as the village expanded, was called Newtown Lane.

OSBORNE-JACKSON HOUSE

Built in 1740 and the headquarters of the East Hampton Historical Society. At 101 Main Street.

POTS-N-KETTLES

A place east of East Hampton's Hook Pond on the beach off Highway Behind the Pond, where blubber was rendered by off-shore whalers into pots and kettles. Off-shore whaling was an established industry in colonial days, the cry "whale off" a call to action for men to launch their whaleboats in pursuit of their valuable quarry. Indians before them had mastered the techniques. Drift whales—beached whales—were viewed as "God's Providence."

PUDDING HILL

In East Hampton Village, south of Wood's Lane, west of Ocean Avenue. Named in 1776 during the Revolution when Mrs. Mary Sanford Miller who lived there threw her pudding down a hill rather than share it with occupying British soldiers.

See the bicentennial plaque at the corner of Ocean Ave. and Route 27.

REUTERSHAN PARK

In the center of East Hampton Village. Named for an early South Fork family.

SAYRE'S PATH

In Wainscott, linking the Montauk Highway with Main Street, named for an original settler family. Thomas and Job Sayre were members of the group who left Lynn, Massachusetts in 1640, landed in North Sea and founded Southampton. Matthew Sayre (1735-1819) fought in the Revolution with Colonel Smith's Regiment.

SEABURY CREEK

A northern tongue of Georgica Pond and the eastern boundary of The Creeks extending almost to the Montauk Highway. Samuel Seabury (1873-1958) was a New York Supreme Court judge who fought municipal corruption in Manhattan in the 1930s. He owned property now encompassed within Georgica Close.

In 1999, his stately house on five acres on Route 114 became the local chapter of The Nature Conservancy.

SETH BARNES POINT

After the fighting in "Massachusetts Bay" and "shocked by the bloody scene", scores of East Hampton men capable of bearing arms signed, in 1775, a General Association announcing that they would "never be slaves", that they were united in fighting "oppressive acts of the British Parliament". One signer was Seth Barnes and we assume that he owned the point of land between Georgica Cove and Georgica Pond that bears his name.

SHEEP POUND

A triangular piece of land in East Hampton village between the post office and the Egypt Lane traffic light, so named because it was once a compound for sheep.

SHERRILL AVENUE

Samuel Sherrill, born in Ireland in 1649, arrived in East Hampton due to being shipwrecked, the first of an illustrious family. General Charles Sherrill who died in 1936 was a former ambassador to Turkey. Sherrill Avenue is in East Hampton village, as is Sherrill Road.

SIX POLE HIGHWAY

A pole is a unit of lineal measure equal to five and a half yards. We assume that this was the width of the original road which is north off Merchant's Path, west of Route 114 in East Hampton.

SOAK HIDES ROAD

Connects Springy Banks Road with Three Mile Harbor Road at East Hampton. The "dreen" or drain at the southern end of Three Mile Harbor was a place where cow hides were soaked to soften them for leather workers. Also called Tanbark Creek.

Soak Hides Preserve is a 34-acre open space area which protects the headwaters of the harbor.

STEPHEN HANDS PATH

In East Hampton, leading north from the Montauk Highway, named after Stephen Hand (1635-1693), a descendant of John Hand, born in England, one of the founders of East Hampton. One of the many illustrious family descendants was Learned Hand, Chief Judge of the U.S. Court of Appeals.

TALMADGE CREEK

A northern finger of Georgica Creek visible from the Montauk Highway and named for a 19th century Town Trustee, a member of a very early family to settle in the area. Thomas Talmadge was one of the nine original settlers of East Hampton. His father settled in Southampton in 1642.

TERBELL LANE

Off Ocean Avenue in East Hampton Village. Edward Terbell once owned all of the property along Ocean Avenue to the dunes and created the Sea Spray Inn, a summer resort which burned to the ground in 1978.

TOILSOME LANE

The Old English word *til*, related to till, had many connotations: to plow, to work hard, to cultivate. It's possible that Toilsome Lane in East Hampton Village had its origins in this word which is also similar to Toylesome Lane in Southampton Village (once described as being "at a place called Tilesome") suggesting—perhaps wrongly—excessive toil and trouble. Tilsome probably meant suitable for plowing and cultivating.

TOWN HOUSE

East Hampton's first meeting house and school at 149 Main Street and operated by the village historical society.

TWO ROD HIGHWAY

A rod is an old term of lineal measurement equal to five and one half yards. This road, in Wainscott, joins Sayres Path with Wainscott Northwest Road.

The original road may have been two rods in width.

TYLER HOUSE

Number 123 on Main Street in East Hampton Village. John Tyler (1790-1862) became president in 1841 when President Harrison died. He married Julia Gardiner of Gardiner's Island.

WAINSCOTT

According to Tooker, the name first referred to Wainscott Pond, and was not Indian in origin but from an ancient method of preparing wainscot, that is, oak timbers or boards, an early export from this region.

Ernest Clowes, however, believes that the name was derived from an English town of the same name, the home of the area's first white settler, around 1670, John Osborn. Hand and Topping are also among the very early settlers of the hamlet.

David Gardiner wrote that the name is derived from an Indian named *Way-un-scutt*.

WHOOPING HOLLOW LANE

Links the East Hampton Sag Harbor Turnpike with Two Holes Water Road in East Hampton. Jeannette Edwards Rattray wrote that "Whooping Boy's Hollow" in this area got its name from "a murder of someone whose spirit hovers around the trees there and frightens passers-by".

WIBORG BEACH

At the end of the Highway Behind the Pond. Named for Frank Wiborg (1855-1930), a self-made millionaire who owned 80 ocean-front acres here. His mansion, next to the Maidstone Club, one of East Hampton's largest, was demolished in 1941.

Sarah, one of Wiborg's daughters, married Gerald Murphy, heir to the Mark Cross business. The couple moved to Europe after the First World War and are remembered for their many friends including F. Scott Fitzgerald, Picasso, and Ernest Hemingway.

Mr. and Mrs. Wiborg and Sarah and Gerald Murphy are interred in the South Burying Ground.

WIRELESS ROAD

In East Hampton between Cove Hollow Road and Toilsome Lane. Named for a radio station which, with towers, could relay messages from ships at sea to Western Union in Manhattan. The station closed in the 1930s and two 165-foot towers are gone leaving only the name.

SPRINGS

ACCABONAC

A harbor in Springs off Gardiner's Bay. The first use of this name of Indian origin was in 1651.

A shorter form, Bonack, refers to Springs and East Hampton in general; bonacker is a self-designation for loyal citizens of the locality, many of whom are members of Sons and Daughters of Accabonac. A considerable portion of shore land bordering Accabonac Harbor has been acquired by the Nature Conservancy.

ASHAWAGH

A locality at Hand's Creek, Three Mile Harbor, first spelled *Ashshowale* in 1666. Tooker tells us that the Algonquin word means "land between the branches of a creek." There was extensive proof of Indian settlement in the area, including many shell heaps.

Ashawagh Hall, built in 1884, originally a school house, is now a community center.

BARNES LANDING

Originally from Norfolk, England, the Barnes descendants are widespread and illustrious in South Fork history from the 17th century. Isaac Barnes was one of the founders of East Hampton. The Landing at Gardiner's Bay is at the end of Barnes Hole Road in Accabonac.

CHAPEL LANE

Named for the small St. Peter's Episcopal Chapel close by on Old Stone Highway in Springs. Built in 1881 as the East Side Free Chapel it was, in 1916, deeded to St. Luke's Episcopal Church and the name changed to St. Peter's.

CHARLES PARSON'S BLACKSMITH SHOP

In Springs, near Pussy Pond, built in 1886.

COPECES LANE

An area in Springs which, according to Tooker, means in the Algonquin language, a small harbor, a "place shut in."

CORBIN AVENUE

Austin Corbin, Jr. became president of the bankrupt Long Island Railroad which, in 1870, extended only to Sag Harbor. He extended the tracks to Fort Pond and wished to make Montauk a Port of Entry for ships crossing the Atlantic. He died in 1896 with his dream unrealized.

Corbin Avenue runs south off Three Mile Harbor Road.

DEEP HOLE

An area in Gardiner's Bay off Cape Gerard (Cape Gardiner) in Springs so named because the water here was deep enough to allow oceangoing ships to unload menhaden at a fish-processing "factory" built in 1875 by Benjamin Payne.

DOMINY LANE

In Springs. The Dominy family was one of the founding families of East Hampton (1669) and identified as furniture makers, clock makers, and windmill builders. Hook Mill was built in 1806 by Nathaniel Dominy. A book on the Dominy craftsmen *With Hammer in Hand* was written by Charles Hummel. Floyd E. Dominy, the First U.S. Commissioner of Reclamation, was born in Nebraska on a homestead created by his grandfather in the 1870s and is written about by John McPhee in *Encounters with the Archdruid*.

DONGAN WAY

Off Hands Creek Road in Springs. Thomas Dongan was a colonial governor of New York who, in 1686 during the reign of King James II, legitimized the claims of ownership within East Hampton. The Dongan Patent assures unencumbered access to the high water mark and the free use by inhabitants to ponds and other bodies of water within East Hampton, Southampton and Southold.

FIREPLACE LANDING

Originally a place in Springs where fires were built as signals to Gardiner's Island indicating that someone wanted to cross the Bay, hence, Fireplace. Lion Gardiner owned land here and built a storehouse. In time, it became a minor commercial center.

FLAGGY HOLE ROAD

Off Hog Creek Road running to Gardiner's Bay. Flag, according to W.W. Tooker, is an early name for cattail whose leaves were used by Indians to weave into mats and baskets; flaggy would mean a place where such wetland plants grew. Sadly, purple loosestrife, an invasive in North America, is supplanting native cattails in many areas.

There's a Flagg Avenue in the Ditch Plain area of Montauk.

In Montauk's Hither Woods, east of Waterfence, there's a wetland filled with cattails called Flaggy Hole.

GANN ROAD

Off Three Mile Harbor Road in Springs. Named for John Gann or his daughter Molly Gann, the wife of Joshua Penny, who built a dock on the harbor in 1823.

The boat shop here is affiliated with the East Hampton Town Marine Museum.

GERARD DRIVE

A continuation of Fireplace Road running the length of Cape Gardiner, between the bay and Accabonac Harbor. It bisects a Town park named for Caroline Gerard who was related to former owner Daniel Gerard. In 1770 this area belonged to Benjamin Leek.

GREEN RIVER CEMETERY

In Springs on Accabonac Road. Probably named for Sam Green Miller whose son Emmett sold it to the Cemetery Association in the late 19th century. There's no river in Springs but some local person once visited Green River, Vermont and for some reason the name was connected to the cemetery.

ISLE OF WIGHT ROAD

The original English name for Gardiner's Island..."I, Lyon Gardiner and Mary my wife...went to an Island of my own which I had bought of the Indians, called by them *Monchonock*, by us the Isle of Wight..."

The Gardiners' second daughter, born on the island (1640) was the first English child born in what would become New York State.

The road is off Hog Creek Highway at Fireplace.

JACOB'S FARM

Bought in 2000 by East Hampton Town and Suffolk County. Said to be named after Jacob Schellenger, a very early owner. In Springs, 165 acres.

KINGS POINT ROAD

In Springs, East Hampton Town, in the Hog Creek area. The King family is thought to be the original settlers here in the 17th century. They are associated with the Gardiners of Gardiner's Island and with the trade from Fireplace across the bay. A widespread place name on the South Fork. Kingstown is a locality off Accabonac Road in Springs.

LASSAW PRESERVE

Off Ed Hults Lane and owned by the Town of East Hampton, this 50-acre forest is contiguous with the Springs School Woodland. Formerly owned by Ernestine Lassaw and the abstract expressionist sculptor Ibram Lassaw, born in 1913, who moved to Springs in the 1950s.

LITTLEWORTH

An area at Accabonac, so named because it was thought to have very little value. Also, an area in Southampton (Beers Map, 1894) south of the railroad tracks where County Road becomes Flying Point Road.

LOUSE POINT

A sandy peninsula enclosing East Hampton's Accabonac Harbor. According to one source, the name originated after fishermen from Connecticut caught so few fish that someone proclaimed that there were not enough fish caught to feed a louse.

MAIDSTONE PARK

In 1911, Frederic and Almy Galatin sold 22 acres at Three Mile Harbor to East Hampton Town. One stipulation was that the land would be a public park.

MERRILL LAKE SANCTUARY

A Nature Conservancy holding off Fireplace Road in Springs with frontage on the northern shore of Accabonac Harbor. Named for Merrill Millar Lake, a naturalist who donated this land to the Conservancy.

MOGKOMSKUT

A large boulder, deposited by the glacier, on Hands Creek Road at Three Mile Harbor, the largest rock Tooker ever saw on Long Island. The Indian word means "at the great rock."

MOLLY'S HILL

Now leveled, this site is located in Springs where Fireplace Road and Gerard Drive meet; said to be named for Molly Pharoah (1819-1879), Stephen Talkhouse's mother. Note plaque.

PARSON'S PLACE

Connects Fireplace Road with Old Stone Highway in Springs and named for the Parson family who were agents for and did business with the Gardiners of Gardiner's Island.

POLLACK-KRASNER HOUSE

A national historic landmark which includes the studio once owned by abstract expressionist artist Jackson Pollack and his wife and fellow-artist, Lee Krasner. On Springs-Fireplace Road, overlooking Accabonac Creek.

PUSSY POND

Now a creek which feeds freshwater into Accabonac Harbor in Springs and crossed by a bridge on Old Stone Highway. Tradition has it that the name came from a Parson woman calling for her cat. This area is now a town park and part of the Accabonac Harbor holdings.

Local members of Waterfowl U.S.A. built the wooden bridge, removed phragmites and introduced aquatic birds. Note the plaque to Marvin T. Bushman (1927-1995).

SPRINGS

Or, The Springs, a peninsula north of East Hampton village, noted for its freshwater springs, excellent harbors, pasture, forests and fishing grounds. The *entrepôt* for Gardiner's Island. The original settlers were Chatfields, Hands, Bakers, Millers, and Bennetts. Until the 20th century, Springs was, for Long Island, a remote area with a small population of self-sufficient farmer-fishermen.

The Springs Library was given to the Town by Mrs. Elizabeth Parker Anderson.

SPRINGS GENERAL STORE

Built in 1884 by David Dimon Parsons. At Springs in East Hampton.

TALMADGE FARM LANE

Named for the Talmadge family. Ferris Talmadge (1897-1968) was a master farmer, sawmill owner and author of a pamphlet *The Springs in the Old Days*. Also, Talmadge Lane in East Hampton Village and Talmadge Lane near Wainscott Pond.

THREE MILE HARBOR

The beautiful harbor, opening to Gardiner's Bay, named because the early village of East Hampton is three miles from the head of Three Mile Harbor.

WILL CURL HIGHWAY

In Springs, a short road off Three Mile Harbor Road named for an Indian, Will Curl.

AMAGANSETT AND NAPEAGUE

ABRAHAMS PATH

Off Springs-Fireplace Road in West Amagansett and running south to the Montauk Highway. Named after Abraham Schellinger (1658-1712), a descendant of an original East Hampton settler and one of the founders of Amagansett. His ancestors came from Holland.

ABRAMS LANDING ROAD

Veers off Main Street in Amagansett Village and runs east to

Napeague Bay at the site of the Devon Yacht Club. On old maps it's called Abrahams Landing Road and might be associated with Abraham Schellinger.

AMAGANSETT

In the Algonquin language, the area's name means "at the place of good fishing," i.e., off-shore whale fishing. The original white settler was Nathaniel Baker who arrived in 1680. Other early families were Miller, Hand, Schellenger, Barnes, Conklin and Conkling. Alfred Conkling (1789-1874) became a congressman and in 1852, Minister to Mexico.

Amagansett received national attention in the spring of 1943 when a German submarine landed some would-be saboteurs on the beach. The men, in civilian clothes, took the train to Manhattan but were soon caught. Some were executed as spies.

ART BARGE

A U.S. Navy World War I barge was towed to Napeague Harbor to fulfill founder Victor D'Amico's (1904-1987) dream of creating a broad-based art school that he began in 1955 at Ashawagh Hall in Springs. It's off Napeague Meadow Road in Amagansett.

ATLANTIC DOUBLE DUNES

A two-and-a-half-mile strip of double dunes between Amagansett and East Hampton protected by the Town and the Nature Conservancy containing micro-habitats for dune flora and fauna. Amphibians such as the Fowler's toad, *Bufo fowleri*, dwell within the small freshwater ponds within the swales. A plaque on the south side of Bluff Road at the end of Meeting House Lane reads:

> *In commemoration of Donald Wingate Lamb, 1897-1977*
> *His guiding force and inspiration*
> *made possible the Atlantic Coastal Double Dunes Preserve*
> *Here, where the sea converges with the land*
> *man's spirit takes wing with nature and is refreshed*

BEAMAN'S CREEK

Flows out of the Napeague Meadows into Napeague Harbor. Could be named for Josiah Beaman, an Indian, or after a family name, Beaman, the maiden name of the wife of George Henry Hand. Sometimes called Beeman Creek and habitat for egrets, herons and similar salt-marsh birds.

BENDIGO ROAD

Links Abrahams Landing Road with Cranberry Hole Road near Promised Land and said to be derived from Bend-I-Go due to the soft bog-like soil that made walking difficult.

BLUFF ROAD

In Amagansett, once an old Indian trail that ran along the high bluffs overlooking the ocean. Part of this area is within East Hampton's historic district. Once the "Old Road," the only way to travel to Montauk.

BUNKER HILL ROAD

In Amagansett, off the Montauk Highway, parallel with the railroad tracks. The name has no connection with the famous Revolutionary battle at Boston but rather with a fish called menhaden or mossbunker; these fish were once so numerous that the first settlers used them as fertilizer. In 1872 the first of many "factories" was created at Promised Land (Bunker City) to process the fish which were eventually exterminated.

The name is said to have originated when a farmer covered a field with mossbunkers without plowing them under; the odor of the rotting fish, carried by the wind, made a lasting impression on the villagers.

CRANBERRY HOLE ROAD

Indians ate native cranberries growing in freshwater lowlands such as those at Napeague and Promised Land. Everett Rattray tells us that Cranberry Hole was a pond, ditched and drained to limit mosquitoes. Cranberry Lane links Oceanview Lane with Cranberry Hole Road.

DEVON

A district bounded easterly by Gardiner's Bay, west of Promised Land. Originally called Abraham's Landing. Many of the original East End families came from Devon in England.

EAST HAMPTON TOWN MARINE MUSEUM

On Bluff Road at Amagansett and containing exhibits and artifacts illustrating the history of whaling and commercial fishing.

FLYNN BEACH

At Napeague on the ocean, an East Hampton Town beach named in 2002 for William Patrick Flynn, killed in action in the Vietnam War.

GLADES

An area in Amagansett, the swale between the bluff (Bluff Road) and the dunes. The low land was frequently flooded and reminded earlier inhabitants of the watery Florida Everglades.

There's a Glades Road in Springs between Three Mile Harbor Road and Fireplace Road.

INDIAN WELLS HIGHWAY

The wells, a source of drinking water for Indians, were in the vicinity of Bluff Road in Amagansett, the "place of good water", when that road was a primitive trail.

A plaque on the west side of the highway reads:

> Near this spot at the Welling Springs of Amagansett
> the Indians used to pause to slake their thirst
> when going to or coming off Montauk.
> 1946 L.V.I.S.

LAZY POINT

A low and sandy peninsula reaching into Napeague Harbor from the west, north of Napeague State Park.

One source claims that it was named long ago because some who dwelt here were idle and lacked a work ethic.

MIANKOMA LANE

Runs from Amagansett's Main Street south to Bluff Road. The name is said to be Indian but there's no documentation and it's not in Tooker's book. No doubt the lane took its name from Miankoma Hall, built in 1904 on Main Street.

MISS AMELIA'S COTTAGE

Named for Amelia Schellenger (1841-1930) of Amagansett and located at the corner of Main Street and Windmill Lane. Amelia was a descendant of Jacob Schellinger (many spellings) born in 1625 in Amsterdam. Amelia never married but was a "woman of property." She died in Cairo, New York when she was almost ninety. The house is now a museum.

NAPEAGUE

The long low stretch of beach and swamp that connects Montauk with the rest of Long Island. Most of this area is now the 1,200 acre Napeague State Park. Derived from the Indian word *Nepeake* it signifies, according to Tooker, "waterland." Before the first paved road was built, travel through this so-called strip was arduous because of the heavy sand and swarms of mosquitoes. In ancient times, this lowland was submerged and Hither Hills and Montauk were islands.

During the hurricane of 1938 much of this area was under water. Also, Napeague Harbor, Napeague Meadow Road, Napeague Beach.

NAPEAGUE POND

South of Lazy Point Road. In 1741 Reverend Horton described an Indian encampment here. North of the pond there were once indications of a 17th century Indian "fort" and other signs of aboriginal habitation. Also called Pond of Pines.

PANTIGO

A locality between East Hampton and Amagansett. The word appeared in 1669 when William Edwards gave his daughter land at Pantego.

Tooker claims no Indian origin. He agrees with Henry P. Hedges, the East Hampton historian, that the word probably evolved from "pant I go," based upon some local happening. Sleight says it was an Indian name meaning "vista."

POSEYVILLE

A locality around Handy Lane and Cross Highway in west Amagansett. One version of the name's origin claims that somebody in the Lester family usually wore a flower in the buttonhole of his jacket. His nickname, Posey, spread to his other relations and eventually to the locality.

PROMISED LAND

A locality in western Napeague fronting on Napeague Bay,

once the site of fish "factories" where menhaden (*Brevoortia tyrannus*) were processed for their oil. Suggested by George Conklin as the name for a post office to be situated there in 1879. Reason unknown.

QUAIL HILL

In north Amagansett near Stony Hill Road. The name appears as early as 1690. Deborah Ann Light, in 1989, donated several parcels of land totaling 25 acres in the vicinity to the Peconic Land Trust. Now an organic farm cooperative, one of the original community supported agriculture (CSA) farms in the U.S.

RAM LEVEL

Robert Villani calls it the largest of the few remaining maritime grasslands on Long Island, dominated by little blue stem, wavy hair grass and Indian grass. Within the County Nature Preserve, Hither Woods, north of the Montauk Highway at Napeague. In earlier days rams might have been kept here to isolate them from ewes.

SCHELLENGER ROAD

Links Windmill Lane with Abrahams Path in Amagansett. The original Schellenger on the South Fork was Abraham (1658-1712) whose ancestors were Dutch.

TALKHOUSE WALK

Off Abraham's Path in West Amagansett and named for Stephen Pharaoh (1819-1879), also known as Stephen Talkhouse, a Montaukett Indian who is buried at Indian Fields in Montauk. Note headstone. He served in the Civil War (29th Connecticut Volunteer Regiment) and on whaling ships and later was East Hampton's town messenger and mailman. He was known as a prodigious walker.

TEENY'S HOLE

A marsh or pond at Napeague Beach west of Napeague Meadow Road. Said to be named for an Indian woman who drowned there. Mentioned in the East Hampton Town Records in 1837.

WALKING DUNES

A desolate area in Hither Hills State Park in Napeague between the railroad tracks and the bay. Called the walking dunes because wind-blown sand from disturbed land to the west, at Promised Land, is relentlessly moving east and, Sahara-like, slowly engulfing the oak forest.

WHIP-POOR-WILL STREET

In Amagansett, off Indian Wells Road, opened around 1730. The name, for reasons unknown, was changed to Atlantic Avenue.

WYANDANCH LANE

A road in Beach Hampton off Bluff Road. Wyandanch was one of the four Indian sachems who in 1648 made their marks on a deed for the Town of East Hampton. Job Sayre was one of the witnesses.

Southampton also has a Wyandanch Lane that links Toylesome Lane and Gin Lane.

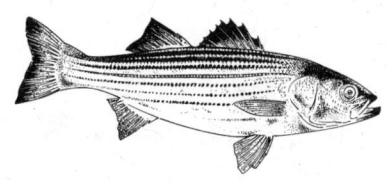

MONTAUK

AGNEW AVENUE

At Ditch Plain in Montauk, C.R. Agnew, a wealthy New York doctor, was a friend of Arthur Benson who, in 1879, bought most of Montauk and invited some of his close friends to build summer homes in a conclave known as the Montauk Association. Stanford White (1853-1906) and Frederick Law Olmstead (1822-1903) were engaged to build the houses.

AMSTERDAM

In October 1867 the steamer *Amsterdam* was wrecked on

the beach some two miles west of the Montauk Lighthouse, directly east of Deep Hollow Ranch. A favorite place for surfcasters.

BENSON DRIVE

Arthur W. Benson, a real estate speculator, was once (1879) the sole owner of Montauk. Benson Drive in Montauk runs parallel with Route 27. Benson dreamed of making the area a hunting and fishing resort but died before those plans materialized. Some of Benson's holdings were later sold to the Long Island Rail Road which, in 1895, extended its tracks to Fort Pond Bay because it was thought that the bay would become a port for trans-Atlantic ocean liners.

BENSON POINT

In Montauk at Ditch Plain. In 1879 Arthur Benson, a millionaire sportsman from Brooklyn, bought all of Montauk (except the federally owned lighthouse and life saving stations) for $151,000 from "The Proprietors" who'd held the land since 1712. This purchase abrogated a 1660 agreement with the Indians giving them and their heirs the right to live on the land.

BENSON RESERVATION

Thirty-five acres of high bluffs, dunes and beach south of the intersection of Montauk State Boulevard and Old

Montauk Highway. Owned by East Hampton Town, it's named in memory of Arthur Benson who owned most of Montauk at the turn of the century.

CAMP HERO ROAD

The last public road before reaching the lighthouse. Camp Hero was a World War II military base at Montauk Point. There are abandoned coast artillery bunkers here and other remnants of the army base.

Most of the moorlands area is within the 420-acre Montauk Point State Park.

CAMP WIKOFF

A temporary military camp at Montauk created during the Spanish American War and named for a regular army colonel who died in Cuba. The camp was created to quarantine soldiers sick with malaria, dysentery and yellow fever. Montauk then was unpopulated and remote.

CAPTAIN BALFOUR WAY

A road in the Culloden Point development at Montauk. Balfour was captain of *HMS Culloden* which was wrecked in 1781 off the point.

COCONUTS

A stretch of beach between Ditch Plain and Montauk Point. In the winter of 1893, the schooner *Elsie Fay* was wrecked here. The ship's cargo of coconuts filled the surf, were collected and eaten in various forms by local scavengers.

CULLODEN POINT

On the stormy, gale-driven night of January 23, 1791, His Majesty's ship *Culloden*, a 74-gun frigate went aground near Fort Pond Bay. A large warship of the Revolutionary period, the *Culloden* was 170 feet long and quartered 650 men. Despite heroic efforts in freezing hail and sleet, the ship was abandoned and found her last resting point in the vicinity of a point of land then known as Will's Point. In 1979 the wreck was listed in the National Register of Historic Places. The point is one of the few remaining habitats of the rare blue-spotted salamander, *Ambystoma laterale*.

DEAD MAN'S COVE

At the beach at Ditch Plain at Montauk. The traditional story indicates that the dead were Shinnecock Indians who drowned trying to save the *Circassian*, wrecked off Southampton in December 1876. Some bodies were carried east and washed ashore at the cove.

DEEP HOLLOW RANCH

Originally named Third House, built in 1747, when it was literally the house of a shepherd who watched over thousands of sheep, cattle and horses which grazed during the summer months. It became quarters for army officers during the Spanish American War and, in 1936, a dude ranch. Now a part of Theodore Roosevelt County Park.

DE FOREST ROAD

Robert W. de Forest (1848-1931) was head of the Southern Pacific Railroad. He gave the American Wing to the Metropolitan Museum of Art (he was a trustee) in Manhattan.

De Forest Road, east of Ditch Plain in Montauk is part of the once-exclusive Montauk Association area created in the 1880s by architect Stanford White who designed many of the houses and a club house which, in 1933, was destroyed by fire.

DEVIL'S CRADLE

A deep ravine in Montauk's Hither Woods carved by the glacier.

DITCH PLAIN

A locality at Montauk derived from *Choppauhshapaua-gausuck*, which, according to Tooker, was the outlet (a ditch so-called) south to the ocean for Great Pond (now Lake Montauk).

DURYEA AVENUE

Off Flamingo Road in Montauk. Duryea, or Duryee is an old and distinguished South Fork name. Colonel Abram Duryee commanded the Fifth New York Regiment in the Civil War and the unit was called the Duryee Zouaves. Hiram Duryea served with the same regiment and became a brigadier general.

DUVAL PLACE

At Ditch Plain in Montauk, named for Guy DuVal, a friend of Arthur Benson, whose house here was designed by Stanford White.

ELISHA'S VALLEY

A low area, between Fresh Pond in Montauk and the high ground north of the old highway near Hither Hills State Park. Elisha was an Indian who lived there around 1870.

FATTING FIELDS

The name for an area close to Oyster Pond in Montauk that was fenced in from the common pasture land. Here, cows and calves were protected from bulls and given extra food.

FIRST HOUSE BURYING GROUND

Off Cemetery Lane, north of the Old Montauk Highway within the western section of Hither Hills State Park. A monument reads

> *Site of First House, Montauk.*
> *This house was built around 1744, rebuilt in 1797*
> *and burned in 1909. The keepers of the cattle lived*
> *in the house for many years.*

The house, together with Second House and Third House were the homes of the shepherds who tended the sheep, cattle and horses when Montauk was grazing land.

In this small burying ground are headstones for Jacob Hand, Mary Hedges and, among others, two men named Hedges.

FORT HILL ROAD

In Montauk, off the highway east of the village, running to the high ground overlooking Fort Pond Bay. Note the historic marker which describes the original Indian "fort."

FORT POND BAY

When the first settlers came to this region, they found a Montauk Indian "fort" overlooking the bay that would bear that name—as well as Fort Pond Hill, a burial place. The fort, actually a stockade, was built as a haven for women and children during war.

GIN BEACH

Located at Montauk between Shagwong Point and Culloden Point. In times past the area was a gin (from gin fence), a holding place—a corral—for cattle and other livestock to graze during the summer.

GOFF POINT

The point that is on the eastern outlet of Napeague Harbor to Gardiner's Bay, named for William Goff, an English judge who had condemned Charles I of England to death and had fled to the New World to save his own head. Tradition has it that he landed in this area, then left for New England.

GRAVESEND AVENUE

North of Montauk Downs State Park off Fairview Avenue. Named for one of two cemeteries for soldiers returning from Cuba who died of malaria and typhoid fever at Camp Wikoff following the Spanish American War (1898).

GUNNUNKS

A swamp in the North Neck at Montauk, midway between Fort Pond and Culloden Point. Tooker tells us that a variant of the Indian word means "tall" and was associated with a squaw called Lucy Gunnunk.

HOYT PLACE

At Ditch Plain in Montauk. Alfred M. Hoyt, a friend of Arthur Benson, who once owned most of Montauk. The Hoyt house was designed by Stanford White.

INDIAN FIELD

East of East Lake Drive in Montauk, including an Indian cemetery and Indian Field County Park which encompasses Big Reed Pond.

An early agreement to define landholding identified land already cultivated by whites as "old ground," that used by Indians as "Indian fields."

KETTLE HOLE ROAD

At Montauk off Flamingo Road, kettle holes are depressions in the land created by blocks of ice that remained after the retreat of the glacier. When they melted, they left kettle-shaped holes which collected water, became lakes, ponds and depressions that over thousands of years accumulated humus to become bogs.

KIRK PARK

In Montauk Village between the highway and Fort Pond. A plaque reads:

> Dedicated to the memory of
> Major General Norman T. Kirk
> USA 1888-1960.
> Surgeon General of World War II,
> Village Doctor, Fisherman, Friend.
> Montauk Village Association

LAKE MONTAUK

Once the largest freshwater pond on Long Island and called Great Pond or Lake Wyandannee, until a channel was dug in 1926 to create a harbor with access to the sea. Nine hundred acres.

MASSACRE VALLEY

A low area east of Fort Hill in Montauk associated with the legend of a fight (1653) between local Montaukett Indians and invading Narragansetts from across the Sound. Several Montauketts were killed and a bride made prisoner. She was later ransomed with help from Lion Gardiner.

MIMOSA BEACH

On the ocean in Montauk Village at South Edison Ave.

Named for a bar, The Mimosa Cafe, (once called The Pirates Den) that was replaced by Nick's, a motel.

MONEY POND

Close to Montauk Point. The name could have originated because of the belief that pirate treasure is buried here.

MONTAUK

Montauk Point was called *Fischers Hoek* on a 1655 map drawn by Nicholaes Visscher of Amsterdam.

An Indian deed refers to *Meuntacut* "high land", one of many variants. Tooker believed that the Indian word referred to a fort or fortified place—that is a stockade created by the early Indians. Such a fort, still standing in 1662, was located on Fort Pond overlooking Fort Pond Bay.

The Dongan Patent—from Governor Dongan in 1686 gave the 12 Trustees of the Town of East Hampton the right to manage the land rights to this large tract, most of it once called "the Hither End."

MONTAUK DOWNS

A prairie on which early settlers grazed their livestock. The name is said to be derived from The Downs of Sussex in England. Part of this area is now Montauk Downs State Park.

There was an Army hospital here after the Spanish American War (1898).

MONTAUK LIGHTHOUSE

One of the first acts (1792) of the first Congress was to initiate the building of this lighthouse which began to operate in 1797. Built on the high rise at the point on land that, according to W. W. Tooker, was called *Wamponamon* (1661) meaning "at the east". The first keeper was Jared Hand.

Close to the lighthouse, overlooking the ocean, is the Lost at Sea Memorial, a sculpture by Malcolm Frazier which pays homage to the local commercial fishing community.

Lost at Sea Memorial

MONTAUK MANOR

This Tudor style hotel built by Carl Fisher opened in 1927 as part of his dream to make Montauk a port for ocean liners. The stock market crash of 1929 and Fisher's death ten years later left the hotel abandoned. Since 1986 it has been rebuilt as a hotel and condominiums overlooking Fort Pond on Signal Hill.

MONTAUK MOUNTAIN

An excellent example of a maritime grassland area, west of Montauk Village and Fort Pond, off Second House Road. A Nature Conservancy holding containing the rare bushy rockrose and the more rare Nantucket shadbush.

MONTAUK PLAYHOUSE

Originally the Montauk Tennis Auditorium built in 1928, part of Carl Fisher's vision of a Miami of the north. Since 1999 the building and 4.4 acres is owned by the Town of East Hampton, close to Montauk Manor.

NAVY ROAD

A narrow, originally concrete, road in Montauk built during World War II when the U.S. Navy had a seaplane base on Fort Pond Bay.

NOMINICKS

The high ground where the Napeague strip or isthmus ends and Montauk proper begins. The word is Indian in origin and means "land that is seen from afar." Now part of Hither Hills State Park.

OGDEN'S BROOK

Or Ogden's Run, a small stream which runs north through Point of Woods, crossing under the highway and into brackish Oyster Pond at Montauk. Mentioned in the Town Records in 1744. John Ogden, the first of an ancient and distinguished family, was a very early settler in 17th century Southampton.

OYSTER POND

This isolated 100-acre coastal pond at Montauk Point is part of Montauk State Park and a refuge for shell drake, black duck and other birds. Also called Lake Munchogue. At times this freshwater pond becomes a tidal estuary. Apparently named because of the abundance of oysters, a staple food of the aborigines.

POINT OF WOODS

A Montauk anomaly: a heavily-wooded and well-watered area of Montauk Point State Park in the Fort Hero area which runs south from the highway to the bluffs overlooking the ocean. Habitat for the rare blue-spotted salamander, *Ambystoma laterale*.

POTINACK

A hole or deep depression close to the cliffs in Montauk, a mile west of Hither Plain U.S. Life Saving Station, that sometimes filled with water. Tooker believes the Indian word suggested "where the land sinks."

PRESIDENT THEODORE ROOSEVELT COUNTY PARK

In Montauk, formerly called Montauk County Park (1,157 acres including Little Reed Pond). Re-named in 1997 to honor Roosevelt and the soldiers who'd been encamped at Montauk during the Spanish American War.

QUEEN'S HIGHWAY

An old name for part of Montauk Highway, named, in 1711 during the reign of Queen Anne. Later called King's Highway which became the major highway from Brooklyn to the South Fork.

RHEINSTEIN PARK

Near Ditch Plain, in Montauk bordering Shadmoor on the east. Once the estate of Sidney Rheinstein, a member of the New York Stock Exchange.

ROD'S VALLEY

In Montauk, west of Fort Pond Bay in Hither Woods, south of Rocky Point. Named for a black man who lived there in the 19th century.

ROUGH RIDER LANDING

Following the Spanish American War, many American soldiers were repatriated to Camp Wikoff at Montauk, named in memory of Colonel Wikoff who had died in Cuba. Montauk at that time was a remote area and the purpose of the encampment was to hold the troops in isolation to prevent any spread of yellow fever to the public. One unit that disembarked was known as the Rough Riders. Theodore Roosevelt was an officer of this regiment (not the commander) and launched his campaign for governor of New York from this encampment. Here, President Taft visited the returning veterans.

ROYAL OAK WAY

In the Culloden Point development in Montauk named for a British warship of 74 guns that visited Gardiner's Bay during the Revolution.

SECOND HOUSE LANE

In Montauk Village. Montauk, until the start of the 20th century, was a summer gazing ground for sheep and cattle. The original house was built in 1746 close to Fort Pond and was the home of a shepherd who tended stock brought to the peninsula for the summer grazing. The house is now a museum.

SHADBUSH ROAD

Early Long Island settlers noticed that when a small gray-barked shrub bloomed it was time for the alewife and shad to swim back to streams where they were born, that it was time to fish. The shrub (*Amelanchier canadensis*) was thus called shadbush. Another name, juneberry, refers to the fruit used in jams and jellies.

In Montauk, Shadbush Road is west of Flamingo Road close to the end of West Lake Drive.

SHADMOOR STATE PARK

A 98-acre ocean-front area near Montauk Point with a half-mile coastline and named because of the moorland character of this high and windswept land. Shad refers to the shadbush shrub. Contains the rare sandplain gerardia (*Agalinus acuta*), an endangered species.

SHAGWONG POINT

Derived from the Indian word *shagwonggonac* and similar variants. Tooker has difficulty with the word and feels that it may have originated from a word meaning "place on the side of a hill." At one time, there were Indian huts on the side of Shagwong Hill at Montauk.

Off the point, there are rock reefs known as Shagwong Reef.

SHEPHERD'S NECK

A point of land on the west of Lake Montauk near Second House Lane. The first house here was built in 1746 when Montauk was a common grazing ground for sheep and cattle. Nathaniel Talmadge was the first official shepherd here and kept sheep pastured in the locality. The present house, now owned by the Montauk Historical Society, was built in 1797.

SKUNKS HOLE

A tidal pond near Goff Point in Montauk's Hither Hills State Park. The name supposedly originated from the powerful stench of fish processed at Promised Land and on Hicks Island, seen on old maps as Skonk's Hole. Menhaden (bunkers) were brought here by the billions (1850-1898) to be ground up for lubricants and fertilizer.

ST. THERESE OF LISIEUX CATHOLIC CHURCH

French Canadians from Cape Breton Island formed the first Catholic community in Montauk. The church—The Church of the Little Flower—celebrated its first Mass in 1930 and is named for the French Saint Therese of Lisieux (1873-1897) of the Carmelite Order. Father Albert Dolan, a Carmelite, was instrumental in the creation of the church with financial aid from many individuals and The Montauk Beach Company including its founder, Carl Fisher.

The church was built in 1929-30, designed by McKenna and Irving.

STEPHEN TALKHOUSE PATH

In Montauk's Hither Woods that is part of the Paumonok Path maintained by the East Hampton Trails Society. (See Talkhouse Walk.)

STEPPING STONE POND

South Lake Drive now covers the stepping stones that once allowed passage across the southwestern shore of Lake Montauk near Osborne's Island.

THIRD HOUSE

Built in 1747, the original building was the home of keepers who looked after cattle and other livestock. A newer building rose in 1806 and is part of Theodore Roosevelt County Park between Oyster Pond and Lake Montauk. Teddy Roosevelt was quartered here after the Spanish American War when

Montauk was a quarantine camp for soldiers from Cuba, sick with malaria and yellow fever.

TURTLE HILL

An early name for the high ground at Montauk Point which became, in 1795, the site of the 80-foot-high lighthouse. Jared Hand was the first lighthouse keeper. Called *Wamponamon* by the Indians. Turtle Cove is just south of the Point.

TUTHILL'S POND

In Montauk on Tuthill Road near Fort Pond Bay. The Tuthill name is widespread on the South Fork. Joshua Tuthill, born in 1732, served in Colonel Josiah Smith's regiment of Minute Men, Suffolk County, during the Revolution.

Montauk Lighthouse at Turtle Hill

WATERFENCE

The name of a fence—which ran into the water at Napeague Bay—to keep cattle pastured in Montauk. The name now applies to an area along Napeague Bay close to the Walking Dunes and Fresh Pond.

WILL'S POINT ROAD

In the Culloden Point development at Montauk. Will was a Montaukett Indian.

ISLANDS

BLOCK ISLAND

The island is the end of the central geologic spine—the Ronkonkoma Moraine—that runs through the center of Long Island and the South Fork. A submerged remnant connects the island with Montauk. Sighted, in 1616, by Adrian Block.

CEDAR ISLAND LIGHTHOUSE

Built in 1839 by the federal government to guide ships into Sag Harbor until 1934. A fog bell was installed in 1870. Previously on a two-acre isle covered by cedar trees, but now on Cedar Point. A sandbar created in the 1938 hurricane connected it to the peninsula. Acquired by Suffolk County in 1967 and now in the National Register of Historic Places.

FISHERS ISLAND

Tooker tells us that Indians called it *Munnawtawkit*, a word that is the origin of menhaden, a small, oily fish used as a fertilizer.

GARDINER'S ISLAND

Manchonack was the Indian name for Gardiner's Island so identified in the Indian deed of 1639 to Lion Gardiner. The island was known as a place where a large number of Indians had died "of a distemper"—Tooker suggests yellow fever. Gardiner came to the 3000-acre island a year before the settlers from Lynn, Massachusetts landed at North Sea. Mary Gardiner, Lion's daughter, was the first child of English parentage to be born in New York State.

Once called—on very old maps—*L'Isle du Jardinier*, the island of the gardener. Lion Gardiner called it the Isle of Wight. In 1640 it was called Luyteant Island. Until it became part of New York State after the Revolution, the island was an independent Manor or Lordship under English law and conferred by royal patent.

Julia Gardiner, in 1844, married John Tyler, the incumbent

President of the United States. Two of her sons served in the Confederate Army; one, John Alexander Gardiner, is buried in East Hampton.

Bostwick

A harbor, a bay, a forest and a creek on Gardiner's Island. The name is said to be derived from an early overseer who worked for Lion Gardiner or one of his descendants.

Cartright Island

Or Cartright Shoals, the southern extension of Gardiner's Island. In 1872, B.C. Cartright established the first menhaden (a fish) processing "factory" at Promised Land, in Napeague. Habitat of the roseate tern, an endangered species.

Fort Tyler

Now destroyed—used for target practice by U.S. pilots during World War II—it was built in 1898 on a small island that once was connected to Gardiner's Island by a narrow spit. The fort was named for Julia Gardiner Tyler who married President John Tyler in 1844 while he was in office. A lighthouse once occupied the site and it's been known as North Point, Gardiner's Point and The Ruins.

GREAT GULL ISLAND

Seventeen miles northeast of Montauk Point, this 17-acre island is an important breeding colony for endangered sea birds such as roseate terns. From 1898 to 1948 it was federal property and the site of Fort Michie, an artillery position. Now owned by the Museum of Natural History, the uninhabited isle is a haven for terns, called "mackeral gulls" by fishermen, hence the name. Some terns winter as far away as South America.

GULL ISLAND

A five-acre island in Three Mile Harbor once known as Dayton's Island.

HICKS ISLAND

Between Goff Point and Lazy Point and part of Napeague State Park. Now deserted, it was the site of one of the Promised Land "fish factories". Hicks is a very early and distinguished South Fork name. Joseph Hicks (1694-1755) arrived in East Hampton in 1720. A preserve for the now threatened least tern, *Sterna antillarum*.

LONG ISLAND

In 1613-14 Adrian Block sailed around the island and his charts were used by William Blau to create, in 1635, a map in which he called Long Island *Matouwacs*, an Algonquian word believed to mean Island of the Periwinkle. In 1656 Nicholaes Visscher used the words Lange Eyland.

OSBORNE'S ISLAND

The island in the southeast area of Lake Montauk.

PAUMANOK

A name for the whole of Eastern Long Island. The first use of the word was in 1639, in the Indian deed for Gardiner's Island where it was spelled *Pommanocc*.

Tooker's belief is that the word means "land of tribute", that eastern Long Island was under tribute by the Pequots and later white settlers. He cites an agreement made in 1637 between Indian leaders of Long Island and the original Dutch and English colonial authorities.

There's a Paumanok Lane off Old Sag Harbor Road in Bridgehampton.

Also, the 125-mile hiking trail, nearly completed, which runs from Rocky Point in Brookhaven to the Montauk Lighthouse. The wild and varied Paumanok Path has been the result of the dedication of numerous groups and municipalities including the Southampton and East Hampton Trails Preservation Societies, Group for the East End and the Long Island Trail Lovers Coalition.

Plum Island Lighthouse

PLUM ISLAND

Northeast of Gardiner's Island, this 850-acre island was the site of Fort Terry from 1898 to 1954. Now a controversial center for the study of animal diseases and a Bio-Hazard Level 3 facility under the Department of Agriculture. Named for the abundance of beach plums. Efforts are underway by local conservationists to have the island designated as a wildlife preserve. The island hosts an astonishing variety of bird species, including oystercatchers, green-winged teals, many types of heron and the rare northern harrier. It is also one of the most significant sites for seals on the east coast and has one of its last truly virgin beaches.

RAM ISLAND

A small privately-owned island in Bullhead Bay connected by a bridge to Sebonic Inlet Road. The name most likely is derived from the practice of isolating rams from ewes after the breeding season.

ROBINS ISLAND

Pelletreau tells us that in 1665 an Indian deed referred to it as *Anchannock*, in English, Robert's Island. The second owner was James Farrett, an agent for the Earl of Stirling who selected it as part of 12,000 acres that he was awarded. It was sold and resold many times, more recently in 1881 to a group of sportsmen who used it as a hunting preserve. The 435-acre island is a habitat for the endangered Eastern Mud Turtle, *Kinosternon subrubrum*. Bought in 1994 by Louis Moore Bacon.

SEDGE ISLAND

Sedge is a type of maritime grass *(Cyperus polystachyos)*. The low island is close to the outlet of Three Mile Harbor and appears on old maps as Penny's Sledge Island. Joshua Penny had been impressed into the British Navy and during the War of 1812 was arrested for suspected local sabotage and sent to prison. His story was published in 1815 as *The Life and Adventures of Joshua Penny*.

The island, across from Sammis Beach Road, is mostly owned by East Hampton Town.

SHELTER ISLAND

From the Indian word *Manhansack* or *Ahaquash* or *Awamock* which means "an island sheltered by islands." Once called Farrett's Island for James Farrett who, in 1637, received the island from the Earl of Stirling. The Sylvester family were the sole owners then, in 1695, selling portions to William Nicholl and George Havens.

Coecles Harbor

Also Coechles, Cocckles, Coeckles' Harbor between Mashomack and Rams Head in Shelter Island. The name's origin is most likely related to a small mollusk whose abode is the "quarterdeck" or "boat shell" so common in these waters. The settlers in 1652 probably named the bay for the multitude of cockles found there, the name then in Middle English being *cockille*.

Duvall Road

On Shelter Island off North Ferry Road. The Duvall family owned a grocery store here around 1893.

Ralph Griffing Duvall (1861-1941) helped organize the Shelter Island Historical Society and in 1932 published *The History of Shelter Island*.

Havens House

On Shelter Island on Ferry Road. Named for James Havens, a sea captain and American patriot who built the house in 1743. It served as a school and post office and in 1968 became the home of the Shelter Island Historical Society.

Jonathan Nicholl Havens (1757-1799) graduated from Yale, served in the State Assembly for many years and was elected to three terms in Congress.

Havens House, Shelter Island

North Ferry, Shelter Island to Greenport route

Jennings Point

On Shelter Island jutting into Southold Bay. Named for Morancy P. Jennings. Also called Rocky Point and Quinipet because of five glacial erratics deposited there.

Mashomack

A point of land at the south of Shelter Island opposite Sag Harbor derived from an Indian word with many variants: *Meshomuk, Mashomuk*, etc. Tooker's belief is that the word means "where they go by boat", actually by dugout canoe from the Indian settlements at Sag Harbor, Three Mile Harbor and Gardiner's Island.

This 2,000-acre peninsula was for many years a hunting preserve and is now a Nature Conservancy holding which supports a large population of nesting ospreys.

Rams Head

On Shelter Island, almost an island, joined to high ground by a narrow causeway that is occasionally submerged.

The Rams Head Inn, built in 1929 was, in 1947, the three-day meeting place of genius-level physicists to discuss openly the implications of atomic energy and quantum mechanics in the post-war world. Some of those present were Richard Feynman, Hans Bethe and J. Robert Oppenheimer.

Rams Head was most likely named by early settlers who chose necks to segregate rams, hogs and bulls from their female counterparts.

Sachem's Neck

Part of one quarter of eastern Shelter Island between Shelter Island Sound and Coecles Harbor bought in 1695 by William Nicoll. W.W. Tooker tells us that the name did not come from a local Indian sachem but from one called Ambusco from Southold who was given permission to remove himself with his family to this new locality. A sachem is a chief.

Sylvester Manor

On Shelter Island and named for Nathaniel and Grissel Brinley Sylvester who, in 1652, arrived from England. The original manor house was replaced in 1735. Boxwood from this estate is said to be the original 17th century source for eastern Long Island. Close to the manor is a small family burial ground where one may view the headstone and epitaph of Nathaniel.

Turkon's Neck

A peninsula on the south of Shelter Island named after an Indian called Turkyman.

STAR ISLAND

Originally called by its Indian name *Munchog*, an island in "Great Pond" at Montauk. The word, according to Tooker, means an "island of rushes", a place where early English settlers mowed rushes and grass for their livestock.

In the 1920s Carl Fisher (1874-1939), the flamboyant developer whose aim was to make Montauk a sort of Miami Beach, opened Great Pond to the ocean and renamed it Lake Montauk. The dredged soil was used to link the island to the mainland which greatly enlarged the island. In 1929, the Montauk Yacht Club was built, a rendezvous for the ultra-rich including J.P. Morgan, the Fords and the Vanderbilts. Florenz Ziegfeld once owned an estate on the island. The U.S. Coast Guard maintains a station there.

TERN ISLAND

A 50-acre island adjacent to Cow Neck in Southampton, once part of The Port of Missing Men. In 2004, owner Louis Bacon granted a conservation easement to The Nature Conservancy. The island supports piping plover, ospreys and seabeach knotweed; the creeks around the island support eelgrass. Named for the least tern.

WOOD TICK ISLAND

A small island inside the entrance of Accabonac Creek acquired by the Nature Conservancy in 1971, known in early days as Edwards Hummock. Edwards, an early settler name, is widespread on the South Fork.

EAST END HISTORICAL SOCIETIES AND MUSEUMS

Old Schoolhouse Museum
Quogue Historical Society
90 Quogue Street
Quogue, NY 11959
(631) 653-4224

Hampton Bays Historical and Preservation Society
PO Box 588
Hampton Bays, NY 11946
(631) 728-0887
www.hamptonbayshistoricalsociety.org

Shinnecock Nation Cultural Center and Museum
100 Montauk Highway
Southampton, NY 11969
(631) 287-4923
www.shinnecockmuseum.org
www.shinnecocknation.com

Water Mill Museum
41 Old Mill Road
Water Mill, NY 11976
(631) 726-4625
www.watermillmuseum.org

Southampton Historical Museum
17 Meeting House Lane
Southampton, NY 11968
(631) 283-2494
www.southamptonhistoricalmuseum.org

Bridgehampton Historical Society
2368 Montauk Highway
Bridgehampton, NY 11932
(631) 537-1088
www.bridgehamptonhistoricalsociety.org

Children's Museum of the East End
376 Bridgehampton Sag Harbor Turnpike
Bridgehampton, NY 11932
(631) 537-8250
www.cmee.org

South Fork Natural History Museum and Nature Center
377 Bridgehampton Sag Harbor Turnpike
Bridgehampton, NY 11932
(631) 537-9735
www.sofo.org

Sag Harbor Historical Society
PO Box 1709
Sag Harbor, NY 11963
(631) 725-5092
www.sagharborhistoricalsociety.org

John Jermain Memorial Library
Sag Harbor History Room
201 Main Street
Sag Harbor, NY 11963
(631) 725-0049
www.johnjermain.org

The Custom House
912 Main Street
Sag Harbor, NY 11963
(631) 725-0250

Ladies' Village Improvement Society of Sag Harbor
PO Box 2222
Sag Harbor, NY 11963
(631) 725-7984

Sag Harbor Fire Department Museum
46 Church Street
Sag Harbor, NY 11963
(631) 725-0779

Sag Harbor Whaling & Historical Museum
200 Main Street
Sag Harbor, NY 11963
(631) 725-0770
www.sagharborwhalingmuseum.org

Shelter Island Historical Society
Havens House
16 S. Ferry Rd.
Shelter Island, NY 11964
(631) 749-0025

East Hampton Historical Society
101 Main Street
East Hampton, NY 11937
(631) 324-6850
www.easthamptonhistory.org

Home Sweet Home Museum
14 James Lane
East Hampton, NY 11937
(631) 324-0713

Ladies' Village Improvement Society of East Hampton
95 Main St.
East Hampton, NY 11937
(631) 324-1220
www.lvis.org

Springs Historical Society
PO Box 1860
East Hampton, NY 11937

Ambrose Parsons House
Springs-Fireplace Road
Springs, NY 11937

Amagansett Historical Association
Montauk Highway at Windmill Lane
Amagansett, NY 11930
(631) 267-3020

The East Hampton Town Marine Museum
301 Bluff Road
Amagansett, NY 11930
(631) 267-6544

Montauk Historical Society
Montauk Point Lighthouse
2000 Montauk Highway
Montauk, NY 11954
(631) 668-2544
www.montauklighthouse.com

Montauk Historical Society
Second House Museum
Montauk Highway (west end of village)
Montauk, NY 11954
(631) 668-5340

Third House Museum
Theodore Roosevelt County Park
Montauk Highway
Montauk, NY 11954
(631) 852-7878

RIVERHEAD AND NORTH FORK

Hallockville Farm Museum
and Folk Life Center
6038 Sound Avenue
Riverhead, NY 11901
(631) 298-5292
www.hallockville.com

Suffolk County Historical Society and Museum
300 W. Main St.
Riverhead, NY 11901
(631) 727-2881
www.suffolkcountyhistoricalsociety.org

Mattituck-Laurel Historical Society and Museums
Main Road (Route 25)
Mattituck, NY 11952
(631) 298-5248
www.mlhistoricalsociety.org

Southold Historical Society
54325 Main Road
Southold, NY 11971
(631) 765-5500
www.southoldhistoricalsociety.org

Horton Point Lighthouse and Nautical Museum
1 Lighthouse Road
Southold, NY 11971
(631) 765-5500

Southold Indian Museum
1080 Main Bayview Road
Southold, NY 11971
(631) 765-5577
www.southoldindianmuseum.org

East End Seaport Museum and Marine Foundation
Box 624
Greenport, NY 11944
(631) 477-2100
www.eastendseaport.org

Railroad Museum of Long Island
440 4th St.
Greenport, NY 11944
(631) 477-0439
www.rmli.us

Stirling Historical Society and Museum
319 Main Street
Greenport, NY 11944
(631) 477-3026

Oysterponds Historical Society Museums
The Museum of Orient and East Marion History
Village Lane
Orient, NY 11957
(631) 323-2480
www.oysterpondshistoricalsociety.org

SOURCES

Adams, J. Truslow, *History of the Town of Southampton*

Adams, J. Truslow, *Memorials of Old Bridgehampton*

Ash, Jim

Benjamin, Mrs. Samuel

Bottini, Mike

Clowes, Ernest, *Wayfaring,* 1953

Curts, *Bridgehampton's Three Hundred Years*

Daniels, Norton

Davidson, Larry

DeRiggi, Mildred

Duryea, Mrs. John

Duvall, *History of Shelter Island*

The East Hampton Star

Epstein, Barlow, *East Hampton: A History and Guide*

Foster, Debra

Gardiner, D., *Chronicles of the Town of East Hampton*

Gardner, Victoria, Column in *The Sag Harbor Express*

Garro, Tony

Geus, Averill Dayton

Glanz, Mrs. Edward

Good, Bill

Greene, Louise Tuthill

Habib, Susan

Halsey, Abigail Fithian, *In Old Southampton*

Haresign, M., *Water Mill*

Hedges, H.P., *History of East Hampton*

Held, Jean

Haring, Warren

Holden, John

Howell, *History of Southampton*

Keene, Robert, *Observations, The Southampton Press*

Kelsey, Carleton, *Amagansett, A Pictorial History*

Joyce, Peggy

Lee, Madeline, *Miss Amelia's Amagansett*

Lowe, Ron

Lupoletti, Richard

McCaslin, Blair

McGuirk, Mrs. John L.

Mott, Paul

Mulvihill, Jane

Munn, Orson

Nugent, Father Raymond

Oliver, Bernard N.

Peiffer, Steven

Pelletreau and Early, *Southampton Town Records*, Vol. 6

Perricone, Michael

Rattray, Everett, *The South Fork*

Rattray, Jeanette Edwards, *East Hampton History*

Robbins and Strachan, Editors, *Springs, A Celebration*

Sanford, Ann H.

Sleight, Harry

The Southampton Press

The Southampton Trails Preservation Society

Stocker, Margaret

Thorsen, Thomas

Tooker, William Wallace, *Indian Place Names on Long Island*

Tredwell, Mrs. Timothy

Underhill, Lois Beachy

Vielbig, Jean

Villani, Robert, *Long Island*

Ward, John A.

Welch, Richard F.

White, John

Willey, Nancy Boyd

Zaykowski, Joseph and Dorothy

Zebrowski, Dolores

INDEX OF PLACE NAMES

Abrahams Path 171, 179

Abrams Landing Road 171

Accabonac 159, 160, 163, 164, 165, 166, 167, 217

Ackerly Street 55

Actors Colony Road 99, 100

Agawam 11, 15, 17, 19, 21, 22, 26, 29, 30

Agnew Avenue 183

Alewife Dreen 33

Amagansett 31, 62, 126, 135, 143, 171, 172, 173, 174, 175, 176, 177, 178, 179, 180, 222, 229

American Hotel 55, 56

Amsterdam 76, 177, 183, 193

Amy's Lane 133

Anna and Daniel Mulvihill Preserve v, 56, 57, 62, 67, 71

Annie Cooper Boyd House 57, 71

Apaquoque 133, 147

Art Barge 172

Art Village 1, 9

Ashawagh 160, 172

Atlantic Double Dunes 173

Atterbury Road 11, 12

Austin's Pond 107

Azurest 57, 59

Baiting Hollow Road 134

Barcelona Neck 123

Barclay's 100

Barkers Island Road 34, 42

Barnes Landing 160

Bayberry Land 2, 6

Beaman's Creek 174

Beebee Windmill 107

Beecher-Hand House 134

Bendigo Road 174

Benson Drive 184

Benson Point 184

Benson Reservation 184

Big Fresh Pond 33, 34, 36, 38, 39, 42

Bishop's Lane 12

Blank Lane 108

Block Island 205

Bluff Road 173, 174, 175, 176, 177, 181, 222

Bostwick 207

Bowden Square 12

Bower's Lane 12

Boyesen Road 13

Breese Lane 13, 15

Breeze Hill 108

Brickiln Road iii, 15, 56, 58, 68, 72, 73, 83, 86

Bridgehampton 3, 15, 18, 20, 49, 58, 62, 68, 73, 82, 86, 88, 93, 94, 97, 107, 108, 109, 110, 111, 112, 113, 114, 115, 116, 117, 118, 119, 120, 121, 209, 220, 227

Buckskill Road 134

Buell Lane 134

Buffalo Wallow 124

Bullhead Bay 5, 6, 34, 41, 211

Bullhead Lane 109

Bullshead Turnpike 109

Bunker Hill Road 174

Burke Street 58

Burkshire Place 58

Burnett Creek 45

Burnt Point 135

Butter Lane 109

Cadmus Drive 59

INDEX OF PLACE NAMES | 233

Calf Creek 45, 112, 114

Calf Pasture Lane 135

Cameron Beach 46

Camp Hero Road 185

Camp Pond 46

Camp Wikoff 185, 190, 198

Canoe Place 2

Captain Balfour Way 185

Captain's Neck 13, 17, 18, 29

Cartright Island 207

Cedar Island Lighthouse 205

Chapel Lane 160

Charles Parson's Blacksmith Shop 160

Chatfield's Hill 59

Chatfield's Hole 124

Christ Episcopal Church 59

Church of All Angels 3

Church Street 59, 64, 93, 221

Circassian Memorial 3

Civil War Monument 60, 61, 93

Clam Island 60

Clinton Academy 135

Clinton Street 55, 60

Clonmoylan Woods v, 62

Cobb Isle 46

Cobb Road 46, 50

Coconuts 186

Coecles Harbor 212, 215

Cold Spring Pond 2, 3, 6

Conkling's Point 62

Conscience Point 24, 35, 39, 49

Cooks Lane 110

Cooper Lane 63, 136

Cooper's Farm Road 13

Cooper's Neck Lane 14

Cooper Street 63

Copeces Lane 161

Corbin Avenue 161

Corwin Road 100

Corwith Homestead 110

Corwith Windmill 47, 49

Cow Neck 35, 39, 217

Cranberry Hole Road 174, 175

Creeks, The 136, 151

Cross Highway 136, 178

Cross Street 63

Cryder Lane 14

Cuffee Drive 63

Cuffee's Beach 124

Culloden Point 185, 186, 190, 198, 203

Culver Hill 14

Custom House 64, 221

Danz Road 15

David's Lane 136

David White's Lane 12, 15, 27, 28

Davis Creek 36, 41

Dayton's Bay 64

Dead Man's Cove 186

Deep Hole 161

Deep Hollow Ranch 184, 187

De Forest Road 187

Dering Road 65

Devil's Cradle 187

Devon 172, 175

Ditch Plain 163, 183, 184, 186, 187, 188, 191, 197

Divinity Hill 136

Division Street 59, 65, 72, 74, 76, 88, 92, 94, 95, 137

Dodson's Pond 66

Dominy Lane 161

Dongan Way 162

Drew Lane 137

Duke Fordham's Inn 66

Duryea Avenue 188

Duvall Road 212

Duval Place 188

East Hampton 25, 42, 59, 62, 63, 65, 66, 76, 77, 81, 86, 90, 91, 94, 108, 109, 113, 124, 125, 127, 128, 129, 131, 133, 134, 135, 136, 137, 138, 139, 140, 141, 142, 143, 144, 145, 146, 147, 148, 149, 150, 151, 152, 153, 154, 155, 156, 159, 160, 161, 162, 163, 164, 165, 166, 167, 168, 171, 173, 174, 175, 178, 180, 181, 185, 193, 195, 201, 207, 208, 209, 212, 222, 228, 229

INDEX OF PLACE NAMES |235

East Hampton Nature Trail And Bird Sanctuary 137

East Hampton Town Marine Museum 163, 175, 222

East Hampton Village North Burying Ground 138

East Hampton Village South Burying Ground 139

Eastville Avenue 66, 71

Edeson Lane 100

Edwards' Hole Road 125

Egypt Lane 136, 137, 140, 143, 152

Elisha's Valley 188

Ellybrook 125, 130

Emma Rose Elliston Park 36

Fahys Road 100

Fairfield Pond 110

Fatting Fields 188

Ferry Road Cemetery 101

Fireplace Landing 162

First House Burying Ground 189

First Neck Lane 14, 15, 17, 116

Fish Crow Landing 3

Fishers Island 206

Fithian Lane 138, 140

Five Rod Road 141

Flaggy Hole Road 162

Flax Pond 47, 50

Flying Point 12, 45, 47, 53, 165

Flynn Beach 175

Fordune Drive 47

Fordham Road 15

Fore and Aft 67

Fort Hill Road 189

Fort Pond Bay 184, 186, 189, 193, 195, 198, 202

Fort Tyler 207

Foster Beach 67

Foster Street 15

Fowler Street 16, 27, 50

Freetown 141

Frogland 67

Further Lane 141

Gann Road 163

Gardiner-Brown House 141, 143

Gardiner's Island 135, 155, 162, 164, 165, 167, 168, 206, 207, 209, 210, 215

Gary Mac's Way 16

Gay Lane 143

Genissee Swamp 67

Georgica 134, 135, 136, 143, 144, 147, 151, 152, 154

Gerard Drive 163, 166

Gibson Lane 110

Gin Beach 190

Gin Lane 16, 17, 22, 181

Glades 176

Gleason Point 101, 102

Glover Street 68, 69, 88

Goff Point 190, 200, 208

Good Ground 4

Goose Pond 144

Grace Estate Preserve 125, 127

Gravesend Avenue 190

Great Gull Island 208

Great Plains Road 17

Great Swamp 56, 68, 69, 81

Green River Cemetery 164

Green Street 69

Guild Hall 144

Gull Island 208

Gunnunks 190

Halsey Homestead 17, 28

Halsey Neck Lane 13, 17

Hampton House 111

Hand's Creek 126, 131, 160

Hannibal French House 69

Hardscrabble 144

Harry's Lane 69

Havens Beach 70, 93

Havens Cemetery 101

Havens House 213, 221

Hayground 111, 113, 114, 115, 120

Hayne's Pond 111, 112

Heady Creek 17, 18, 21, 26

Hedges Banks 127

Hedges Lane 111

Hempstead Street 71

Herald House 57, 71

Herne Street 36

Herrick Park 145

Herrick Street 18

Hicks Island 200, 208

Highway Behind the Lots 145

Hills Station Road 3, 4, 12

Hill Street 13, 15, 17, 18, 21, 23, 24

Hogoneck Lane 101

Holmes Hill Road 36

Home Sweet Home 86, 145, 222

Hook Pond 138, 145, 146, 147, 150

Hook Windmill 146

Hoppy Toad Hill 71, 80

Horse Mill Lane 19

Howell Street 19

Hoyt Place 191

Hull Lane 112

Hunting Street 19

Huntington Crossway 112

Huntting Lane 137, 146

Indian Field 180, 191

Indian Wells Highway 176

Isle of Wight Road 164

Jacob's Farm 164

Jagger Lane 20

James Lane 145, 146, 150, 222

Janet Creek 101, 102

Jason's Rock 127

Jeffrey's Lane 146

Jehu's Pond 112

Jennings Point 214

Jennings Road 37

Jericho Road 147

Jermain Avenue 67, 72, 73, 85

Jesse Halsey Lane 72

Jessup's Neck 60, 72, 74, 82, 95

Job's Lane 11, 14, 20, 28, 118

Joel Lane 73

John Jermain Library 72, 73, 95

John Jermain's Mill 73

Jule Pond 20

Keewaydin 21

Kellis Pond 112

Kettle Hole Road 191

Kings Point Road 165

Kirk Park 192

Kirk's Place 127

Lafarge's Landing 128

Lake Montauk 81, 188, 192, 200, 201, 209, 216

Lamb's Corner 73

Lassaw Preserve 165

Latham Street 74, 88

Lazy Point 176, 178, 208

Learned Hand's Court 147

Lee Avenue 18, 21

Lenape Road 4

Ligonee 74, 75, 79

Lily Pond Lane 133, 137, 147

Linden Lane 21

Little Noyac 36, 42, 74, 85

Little Plains Road 22, 25

Littleworth 165

Lola Prentice Park 22

Lone Grave Road 128

Long Island iv, v, vi, 4, 5, 20, 21, 34, 37, 42, 50, 55, 63, 64, 65, 68, 71, 74, 85, 89, 92, 94, 113, 115, 127, 128, 129, 130, 161, 166, 168, 177, 179, 184, 192, 199, 205, 208, 209, 216, 224, 230

Long Pond Greenbelt 69, 75, 82, 97

Long Wharf 75

Loper's Path 76

Louse Point 165

INDEX OF PLACE NAMES | 239

Love Lane 76

Luther Drive 48

Lyman Beecher House 148

Magee Street 22, 31, 42

Maguerite Crabbe Greeff Wildlife Sanctuary 37

Maidstone 125, 140, 144, 145, 148, 150, 156, 166

Maidstone Club 140, 144, 145, 148, 156

Maidstone Park 166

Major's Path 29, 37, 38

Mankesack Island 77

Mary's Lane 38

Mashashimuet Park 72, 77, 85

Mashomack 212, 214

Massacre Valley 192

Maunekea Street 102, 103

Maycroft 103

Mcguirk Street 149

Meadow Club, The 22

Meadow Lane 15, 16, 17, 23, 24, 78

Meadowlark Lane 78

Mecox 19, 20, 21, 31, 45, 46, 48, 49, 51, 63, 89, 111, 112, 113, 114, 116, 118

Mecox Dune Preserve 48

Meeting House Lane 23, 30, 173, 220

Merchants Path 113

Merrill Lake Sanctuary 166

Methodist Hill 78

Miankoma Lane 177

Middle Line Highway 78

Militia Green 113

Mill Creek 42, 48, 51, 74, 78, 81

Mill Hill Lane 149

Mill Hill Mill 4

Mill Pond Lane 48

Millstone Brook Road 36, 38, 40, 89

Millstone Road 79, 89

Mimosa Beach 192

Minden 114

Minnesunk Pond 38

Miss Amelia's Cottage 177

Missapogue Court 39

Mitchell Lane 109, 114

Mogkomskut 166

Molly's Hill 166

Money Pond 193

Montauk 4, 5, 6, 7, 8, 9, 12, 15, 22, 41, 46, 49, 52, 81, 89, 110, 113, 115, 117, 121, 134, 137, 147, 151, 153, 154, 161, 163, 171, 174, 176, 177, 179, 180, 183, 184, 185, 186, 187, 188, 189, 190, 191, 192, 193, 194, 195, 196, 197, 198, 199, 200, 201, 202, 203, 205, 208, 209, 216, 217, 219, 220, 222, 223

Montauk Downs 190, 193

Montauk Lighthouse 184, 194, 202, 209

Montauk Manor 195

Montauk Mountain 195

Montauk Playhouse 195

Montrose Lane 114

Morris Cove 33, 79

Morrison Lane 48

Moses Lane 23

Mott's Pond 79

Mountain Laurel Road 23

Mount Misery Road 79

Muchmore Lane 149

Mulford Farm 150

Mulford Lane 79, 81

Mulvihill Pond 81

Munchogue Drive 81

Municipal Building 81

Munn Point 24

Murray Lane 24

Nancy Boyd Willey Park 82

Napeague 81, 171, 172, 174, 175, 176, 177, 178, 179, 180, 190, 196, 203, 207, 208

Napeague Pond 178

Narod Blvd 114

Narrow Lane 16, 114, 115

National Golf Links of America 2, 4, 5, 6, 9

Navy Road 195

INDEX OF PLACE NAMES | 241

Newman Avenue 115

New Light Lane 115, 116

Newtown Lane 63, 136, 145, 149, 150

Nineveh Beach 82

Nominicks 196

Norris Lane 115

Northampton Colony 82

North Haven 52, 70, 77, 85, 99, 100, 101, 102, 103, 104, 105

North Haven Point 101, 104

North Sea 5, 19, 24, 26, 31, 33, 34, 35, 36, 37, 38, 39, 40, 41, 42, 49, 89, 93, 151, 206

Northwest 81, 82, 113, 123, 124, 125, 127, 128, 129, 130, 131, 155

Nowedonah Lane 48

Noyac 33, 34, 36, 37, 38, 40, 41, 42, 43, 55, 58, 60, 67, 69, 72, 74, 78, 79, 81, 82, 83, 85, 89, 92, 94, 95, 96, 97, 100, 104

Ocean Road 107, 111, 112, 113, 114, 115, 116, 117, 118, 120

Ogden's Brook 196

Old Burying Ground 83, 91, 108

Old Field Lane 24

Old Fort 5, 25

Old Fort Pond 5

Old Mill Road 49, 220

Old Southampton Burial Ground 25

Old Town Road 18, 24, 25, 28, 29, 31

Osborne Avenue 25

Osborne-Jackson House 150

Osborne's Island 201, 209

Osceola Drive 5

Otter Hose Company 85

Otter Pond 65, 67, 72, 73, 75, 77, 85

Ox Pasture Road 26, 27

Oyster Pond 188, 196, 201

Palmer Terrace 85

Pantigo 133, 178

Parrish Memorial Hall 26

Parrish Museum of Southampton 26

Parsonage Lane 116

Parson's Place 167

Paul's Lane 116

Paumanok 42, 209

Payne's Creek 85

Peconic 2, 3, 5, 6, 34, 35, 36, 37, 39, 42, 67, 95, 179

Pelletreau Street 26, 27

Pennies Landing 27

Pennypacker Avenue 128

Philips Pond 27

Phoebe Scoy Highway 129

Pierson High School 66, 72, 74, 86

Plum Island 93, 210

Point of Woods 196

Pollack-Krasner House 167

Polles Creek 103, 104

Port of Missing Men, The 39

Poseyville 178

Post Crossing 28, 43

Potash Pond 116

Potinack 197

Pots-N-Kettles 150

Powder Hill 129

Poxabogue 113, 114, 115, 117

Poxabogue – Evergreen Cemetery 117

President Theodore Roosevelt County Park 197

Promised Land 174, 175, 178, 180, 200, 207, 208

Proprietors Lane 49

Pudding Hill 151

Pulaski Street 28

Purgatory 76, 86

Pussy Pond 160, 167

Quail Hill 179

Queen's Highway 197

Quimby Lane 117

Ram Island 211

Ram Level 179

INDEX OF PLACE NAMES | 243

Rams Head 212, 215

Rattlesnake Creek 129

Rebadam Lane 6

Rector Street 88

Redwood 88

Reutershan Park 151

Rheinstein Park 197

Richard L. Fowler Nature Walk 16

Robins Island 211

Rod's Valley 198

Rogers Memorial Library 20, 28

Rogers Street 28, 88

Rosemary Lodge 49

Rose Street 88

Rough Rider Landing 198

Royal Oak Way 198

Ruggs Path 89

Rum Hill 89

Ruth Wales Dupont Sanctuary 13, 29

Ryder's Pond 104

Rysam Street 76, 89, 92

Sachem's Neck 215

Sagaponack 6, 75, 91, 107, 110, 111, 116, 117, 118, 121, 137

Sage Street 59, 91

Sagg Road 91, 97, 114, 118, 120

Sagg Swamp Preserve 118

Sag Harbor 15, 16, 18, 19, 20, 33, 36, 37, 47, 55, 56, 57, 58, 59, 60, 61, 62, 63, 64, 65, 66, 67, 68, 69, 70, 71, 72, 73, 74, 75, 76, 77, 78, 79, 81, 82, 83, 85, 86, 87, 88, 89, 90, 91, 92, 93, 94, 95, 96, 99, 100, 103, 104, 108, 109, 112, 113, 119, 121, 123, 125, 126, 127, 128, 129, 130, 137, 141, 144, 147, 156, 161, 205, 209, 214, 215, 220, 221, 228

Sag Harbor Whaling Museum 20, 90

Sag Harbor Yacht Club 91, 103

Saint Andrew's School 92

Saint James Episcopal Chapel 92

Saint Regis Court 130

Sammis Beach 128, 130, 212

Sam's Creek 118

Sanford Street 29

Sawasett Avenue 119

Sayre Park 119

Sayre's Path 151

Sayre's Pond 50

Scallop Pond Preserve 40

Schellenger Road 179

Scotch Mist Lane 6

Scott Road 37, 40

Scott's Landing Road 40

Scoy's Pond 130

Scuttlehole Road 56, 58, 68, 79, 81, 107, 108, 110, 111, 112, 114, 119, 120

Seabury Creek 151

Sebonac Neck 6

Second House Lane 198, 200

Sedge Island 211

Seth Barnes Point 152

Seven Ponds 47, 50, 51

Shadbush Road 199

Shadmoor State Park 199

Shagwong Point 190, 199

Sheep Pound 152

Shelter Island 7, 65, 70, 100, 101, 103, 104, 134, 212, 213, 214, 215, 216, 221, 227

Shepherd's Neck 200

Sherrill Avenue 152, 153

Shinnecock iii, v, 1, 2, 3, 4, 5, 6, 7, 8, 9, 17, 18, 23, 24, 29, 30, 48, 63, 124, 186, 219

Shinnecock Hills Golf Club 7

Shinnecock Hills Preserve 8

Shinnecock Indian Reservation 1, 3, 5, 8, 18

Shorts Pond 108, 110, 120

Six Pole Highway 153

Skunks Hole 200

Slade Pond 120

INDEX OF PLACE NAMES | 245

Sleight's Hill 78, 92

Soak Hides Road 153

Southampton 1, 2, 3, 4, 5, 6, 7, 8, 9, 11, 12, 13, 14, 15, 16, 17, 18, 19, 20, 21, 22, 23, 24, 25, 26, 27, 28, 29, 30, 31, 34, 35, 36, 37, 38, 39, 41, 42, 43, 45, 46, 47, 48, 52, 56, 66, 72, 83, 86, 87, 89, 93, 97, 107, 108, 111, 113, 116, 119, 137, 141, 151, 154, 162, 165, 181, 186, 196, 209, 217, 219, 220, 227, 228, 229, 230

Southampton Historical Museum 30, 220

South End Burial Ground 25

Split Rock Road 40

Springs 59, 141, 146, 159, 160, 161, 162, 163, 164, 165, 166, 167, 168, 169, 171, 172, 176, 222, 229

Springs General Store 168

Springy Banks 131, 153

Squaw Hill 8

St. Andrew's Dune Church 30

St. Andrew's Road 9

Stanton House 93

Star Island 81, 216

Station Road 50

Stephen Hands Path 126, 131, 134, 144, 147, 153

Stephen Talkhouse Path 201

Stepping Stone Pond 201

Steven Halsey's Path 50

Stock Farm 104

Straight Beach 120

Strong's Lane 120

St. Therese of Lisieux Catholic Church 200

Studio Lane 9

Sugar Loaf Hill 9

Swan Creek 51

Sylvester Manor 216

Talkhouse Walk 180, 201

Talmadge Creek 154

Talmadge Farm Lane 168

Taylor's Creek 30

Teeny's Hole 180

Terbell Lane 154

Tern Island 217

Terry Drive 57, 93

Third House 187, 189, 201, 223

Three Mile Harbor 65, 126, 128, 130, 131, 141, 153, 160, 161, 163, 166, 168, 169, 176, 208, 211, 215

Toilsome Lane 154, 156

Toll Gate 93

Toppings Field Court 120

Toppings Path 97, 120

Towd 36, 40, 41

Towd Point 36, 41

Town House 154

Tredwell Lane 94

Trees Lane 121

Trout Pond 37, 78, 89, 94

Tuckahoe 1, 8, 9, 30, 31, 41

Tuckahoe Hill 31

Tuckahoe Swamp 41

Tucker Mill Inn 4, 9

Turkon's Neck 216

Turtle Hill 202

Tuthill's Pond 202

Two Holes of Water Road 124, 131, 156

Two Rod Highway 155

Tyler House 155

Tyndal Point 104

Umbrella House 94

Union Street 60, 94, 95, 96

Van Scoy Cemetery 131

Villa Maria 51

Villa of Saint Joseph 51

Wainscott 126, 141, 151, 155, 168

Walking Dunes 180, 203

Waterfence 163, 203

Water Mill 18, 38, 41, 45, 46, 47, 48, 49, 50, 51, 53, 79, 89, 111, 220, 228

Water Mill Beach Club 53

Water Mill Community House 53

Wegwagonuck 95

Whalebone Landing 95

Whalers' Church 91, 96

Wheelock Walk 131

Whip-Poor-Will Street 180

White's Lane 5, 41, 42

Whooping Hollow Lane 156

Wiborg Beach 156

Wickapogue 16, 20, 24, 27, 29, 31, 47, 50

Wickatuck Drive 96

Wickatuck Spring 97

Wick's Tavern 121

Widow Gavitts Road 97

Will Curl Highway 169

William Mulvihill Preserve v, 62, 69, 97

Will's Point Road 203

Windmill Lane 4, 22, 25, 31, 177, 179, 222

Wireless Road 156

Wireless Way 42

Wolf Swamp Lane 42

Wood Tick Island 217

Wooley Pond 36, 40, 41, 42, 74

Wyandanch Lane 181

NOTES

I am aware of many omissions in this collection and have little doubt that, because of my want of industry, this effort contains errors, misconceptions and misinformation. With this spirit, I welcome comments from those gentle readers who wish to correct, refine and perhaps add those South Fork place names which, to date, have eluded me.

William Mulvihill

Brickiln Press, LLC
P.O. Box 2772
Sag Harbor, NY 11963